SCIENTIFIC
ASTRO VASTU

A Practical Approach

Theory, Application & Case Studies
For Modern Spaces

Vishal Agarwal

ink Scribe

ink

Scientific Astro Vastu: A Practical Approach

Publisher: Inkscribe Media Pvt. Ltd

ISBN Number: 978-1-966421-59-7

CONTENTS

Preface 5

Chapter 1: Introduction to Astro Vedic and Vastu Shastra............................9

Chapter 2: What is Astro Vedic and What is Vastu Shastra? 13

Chapter 3: How Astro Vedic and Vastu Shastra Are Important
in One's Life 25

Chapter 4: How the Vastu of Land Matters.....................................33

Chapter 5: Why One Needs to Check the Vastu 39

Chapter 6: How Vastu Shastra and Astro Vedic Are Different
but Work Together..45

Chapter 7: The Importance of the Land's Vastu in Shaping
Your Future 51

Chapter 8: Aligning Astro Vedic with Vastu Shastra
for a Harmonious Life..57

Chapter 9: The Role of Vastu in Enhancing Career and Wealth 63

Chapter 10: Vastu and Health: Creating a Harmonious
Environment for Well-being 69

Chapter 11: The Role of Vastu in Relationships and Family Harmony 75

Chapter 12: Vastu for Prosperity and Abundance...........................81

Chapter 13: Vastu and Health – The Vital Connection 89

Chapter 14: Vastu for Prosperity and Wealth 95

Chapter 15: The Impact of Vastu on Relationships 101

Chapter 16: The Role of Vastu in Career and Success 109

Chapter 17: The Science Behind Vastu Shastra and
Astro Vedic Principles 117

Chapter 18: Integrating Astro Vedic with Modern Living 125

Chapter 19: Vastu Shastra and Astro Vedic:
Their Role in the Workplace 131

Chapter 20: Vastu Shastra and Astro Vedic for Homes:
Creating a Harmonious Living Space 137

Chapter 21: Vastu Shastra and Astro Vedic for Workplaces:
Creating Productive and Prosperous Environments 143

Chapter 22: Using Astro Vedic and Vastu Shastra
for Personal Growth and Self-Improvement 151

Chapter 23: The Role of Vastu Shastra and
Astro Vedic in Business and Career Success 157

Chapter 24: The Importance of Vastu Shastra and
Astro Vedic in Health and Well-Being 163

Chapter 25: Harmonizing Your Living Space for Prosperity 169

Chapter 26: An Case Study of Vastu Compliant Office 175

Chapter 27: Conclusion: The Path to Prosperity 181

PREFACE

Every journey has a beginning, a middle woven with challenges and triumphs, and moments of profound transformation that redefine the path entirely. The story of Vishal Agarwal, the author of this book, is one such compelling narrative – a testament to resilience, radical change, and the profound insights that can emerge from the unexpected turns of life.Born in the verdant landscape of Tinsukia, Assam, in 1990, Vishal's formative years were steeped in the dynamic reality of a family navigating the intricate dance of growth, struggle, reaching heights, and enduring various ups and downs. This early exposure to the volatile nature of life and business laid a practical foundation, even as he pursued formal education, culminating in an MBA from the prestigious Narsee Monjee Institute of Management in Mumbai, from which he graduated in 2013.Entering the family business, Vishal embraced the role with intense dedication, quickly becoming a workaholic. He immersed himself in the demanding world of running factories and organizations, learning the intricate mechanics of commerce, experiencing both the harsh realities of struggle and the exhilaration of significant success and financial prosperity. He mastered the art of building and managing, operating within the conventional matrix of achievement. Then, life delivered an extraordinary, life-altering event. A severe car accident – a terrifying plunge of twenty feet that left the vehicle in pieces – should have been a final chapter. Yet, miraculously, Vishal emerged, seatbelt fastened, with barely a scratch, save for a minor spinal injury. Staring back at the mangled wreckage from which he had impossibly escaped, a profound realization dawned: he had been saved by something, someone, powerful beyond comprehension. This near-death experience was not just a physical jolt, but a spiritual awakening, marking the indelible start of his deeply personal journey into faith and unseen energies. The mandatory six months of bed rest that followed, a period previously unimaginable for his relentless pace, became an unexpected gift of time. It was here, away from the clamor of business, that Vishal began to explore the vast realms of spirituality, cosmology, energy flows, rituals, and their deeper significance. This quest for understanding led him to seek deeper wisdom and connect with established spiritual teachings and methods. Under guided study, Vishal delved into the ancient, yet increasingly relevant, disciplines of Scientific Vastu and astrology. It was Astro Vastu, the synthesis of celestial influences and spatial energies, that particularly captivated him, resonating with a surprising clarity. Driven by an innate curiosity and a mind trained in analysis from his business background, he embarked on a rigorous study – collecting data, examining countless life stories alongside house maps and birth charts, and meticulously analyzing case after case. This period of intense study and practical correlation wasn't merely academic; it was the foundation for application. As he began practicing, applying remedies, and observing the tangible results in people's lives, his confidence in the efficacy of these ancient sciences, viewed through a modern, analytical lens, solidified. This book is a culmination of that extraordinary journey – from boardroom to bed rest, from material success to spiritual awakening, from near-fatal accident to dedicated practitioner. Vishal Agarwal brings a unique perspective, combining the pragmatism of a seasoned businessman forged in real-world challenges with the deep spiritual insights gained from a transformative personal crisis and dedicated study. He doesn't just present theories; he shares knowledge tested by experience and validated by observed results. Prepare to explore insights that bridge the seen and the unseen, guided by an author who has walked through the fire and emerged with wisdom to share. His story is embedded within these pages, offering not just information, but the perspective of someone who has personally experienced the profound interconnectedness of life, energy, and destiny.

CHAPTER 1: INTRODUCTION TO ASTRO VEDIC AND VASTU SHASTRA

In the vast expanse of Indian knowledge systems, two ancient sciences have stood the test of time—**Astro Vedic (Vedic Astrology)** and **Vastu Shastra**. Both disciplines have their roots in the Vedas, India's sacred texts, and serve as guiding principles for achieving harmony, balance, and well-being in life. This chapter sets the foundation for understanding these systems—not as superstitions, but as structured sciences deeply ingrained in observation, energy principles, and cosmic alignment.

1.1 THE ORIGINS

Astro Vedic, also known as Jyotish Shastra, is the science of celestial influence on human life. It is based on precise astronomical calculations, the positions of stars and planets, and how these positions correspond to the timing of events in one's life. It seeks to decode the divine blueprint of a person's life, imprinted at the moment of their birth.

Vastu Shastra, on the other hand, is the science of architecture and spatial arrangement. It provides guidelines for designing buildings and environments in alignment with the five elements— earth, water, fire, air, and space—and cosmic energies. This harmony is believed to influence prosperity, health, relationships, and spiritual growth.

Though distinct in their approach, both sciences work on a common principle: the alignment of human life with cosmic and natural energies.

1.2 SCIENCE OR SPIRITUALITY?

While often considered esoteric or religious, both Astro Vedic and Vastu Shastra offer scientific frameworks grounded in observation, mathematics, and empirical logic. For example:

- Astro Vedic uses astronomical data to chart planetary positions and their transitions (dashas, transits).

- Vastu Shastra uses directional forces, energy fields (pranic energy), and geomagnetic influences to guide spatial design.

Modern science increasingly recognizes the influence of energy and environment on human well-being. Concepts like circadian rhythms, geomagnetic sensitivity, and environmental psychology share parallels with these ancient systems.

1.3 THE ROLE IN EVERYDAY LIFE

In daily life, Astro Vedic guides individuals through personalized horoscopes (janam kundalis), identifying strengths, weaknesses, and optimal timing for decisions. From career choices to marriage compatibility, it seeks to optimize life's outcomes.

Vastu Shastra affects where and how we live and work. A poorly designed home may lead to chronic stress, poor health, or financial instability, while a Vastu-compliant space fosters peace, clarity, and abundance.

Together, they provide a **holistic approach to living**—where time (Astro Vedic) and space (Vastu Shastra) work in harmony.

1.4 WHY RELEVANCE TODAY?

In a world where stress, chaos, and uncertainty are increasing, people are turning back to ancient wisdom for solutions. Astro Vedic and Vastu Shastra are being revisited—not just in India, but globally—for their **practical insights** and predictive accuracy.

Modern architects consult Vastu experts during planning. Tech entrepreneurs use Astro Vedic principles to choose auspicious dates for product launches. Individuals look at their planetary periods before making major life decisions.

This revival signals not a regression into superstition, but a recognition of systems that are both **rational and spiritual**, intuitive yet structured.

1.5 THE JOURNEY AHEAD

This book explores how these two disciplines can be integrated, compared, and applied effectively. We will look at their philosophies, their differences, and their intersections. We'll answer key questions:

- Can Vastu enhance the effects of a positive planetary period?

- Can unfavorable planetary influences be mitigated by correcting one's surroundings?

- How do time and space together shape destiny?

The journey begins here—at the intersection of stars and structures, karma and construction, the cosmic and the material.

CHAPTER 2: WHAT IS ASTRO VEDIC AND WHAT IS VASTU SHASTRA?

To truly appreciate the synergy between Astro Vedic and Vastu Shastra, it is essential to first understand the **individual essence** of each discipline. This chapter offers a deeper dive into what these systems are, how they function, and why they remain relevant even in the age of modern science and technology.

2.1 WHAT IS ASTRO VEDIC (VEDIC ASTROLOGY)?

Astro Vedic, or **Jyotish Shastra**, is one of the six Vedangas (limbs of the Vedas), often referred to as the "eye of the Vedas." It is not merely the art of predicting the future, but rather a comprehensive **science of time**, guiding individuals on how to live in harmony with cosmic rhythms.

At its core, Astro Vedic is based on the belief that the positions of celestial bodies at the time of birth can reveal a great deal about one's nature, strengths, challenges, and life path. A natal chart, or **Janam Kundali**, is created using:

- Date of birth

- Exact time of birth

- Geographical location of birth

This birth chart is a snapshot of the sky at the moment you were born. It maps the twelve zodiac signs, nine planets (including

Rahu and Ketu), and twelve houses—each house representing different aspects of life such as career, marriage, health, finance, etc.

KEY COMPONENTS:

- Lagna (Ascendant): Your personality and how the world sees you.

- Rashi (Moon Sign): Your mind, emotions, and inner nature.

- Planetary Periods (Dasha System): Timelines that show the influence of planets over time.

- Transits (Gochar): Movement of planets that affect current circumstances.

Rather than being deterministic, Astro Vedic empowers individuals to make better choices by understanding tendencies and timing life events.

Example: If a person's chart shows a weak Jupiter (the planet of wisdom and finance), they may face delays in education or financial growth. Remedies might include charity, mantra recitation, or timing key decisions when Jupiter is favorably placed.

2.2 WHAT IS VASTU SHASTRA?

Vastu Shastra is the ancient Indian science of architecture and spatial harmony. While Astro Vedic deals with the **dimension of time**, Vastu focuses on the **dimension of space**.

It is based on the principle that **the Earth is a living organism,** constantly interacting with solar, lunar, magnetic, and cosmic energies. A Vastu-compliant space ensures that these energies flow in a way that promotes health, peace, and prosperity.

CORE PRINCIPLES:

- **Five Elements (Panchabhutas):** Earth, Water, Fire, Air, and Space.

- **Sixteen Directions:** Each direction (North, South, East, West, and SSW, WSW, WNW, NNW, ENE, NNE, ESE, SSE, the four intercardinal directions) is associated with specific energies and deities.

- **Center (Brahmasthan):** The core of the house where energies converge. It should be kept open, clean, and uncluttered.

- **Vastu Purusha Mandala:** A metaphysical diagram used as a blueprint for designing spaces, ensuring symmetry and balance.

Example:

- The **kitchen**, associated with the fire element, is ideally placed in the **southeast**.

- **Toilets,** representing waste disposal, should not be in the **northeast**, as it is a spiritually sensitive zone associated with water and clarity.

Homes, offices, temples, and even cities can be designed using Vastu principles. When built correctly, such spaces foster well-being, clarity of mind, and material success.

2.3 THE OBJECTIVE OF EACH DISCIPLINE

Feature	Astro Vedic	Vastu Shastra
Domain	Time	Space
Focus	Personal destiny and timing	Physical environment and energy flow
Tools	Birth chart, planetary positions	Architectural blueprints, directional analysis
Aim	Align life decisions with cosmic timing	Align space with natural energy principles

2.4 WHY DO PEOPLE STILL USE THEM TODAY?

Despite centuries of advancement, modern individuals often find themselves facing **unseen obstacles**—be it in relationships, finances, or health. Many turn to Astro Vedic and Vastu not for superstition, but for **clarity and control**.

- A startup founder may consult an astrologer before launching a product.

- A family may seek Vastu advice before purchasing a plot or building a house.

- A couple planning a wedding may pick a date after matching horoscopes.

The key reason these sciences still hold value is their **ability to provide direction**—offering a roadmap in moments of uncertainty.

2.5 Misconceptions and Clarifications

It is important to differentiate scientific application from blind superstition:

Astro Vedic is not about fear or fatalism—it's about timing and potential.

Vastu Shastra is not about blindly demolishing homes—it's about adjustment, balance, and energy correction, often achievable with minor changes.

Modern practitioners increasingly use software, satellite mapping, and structural engineering tools to enhance accuracy and applicability, blending tradition with technology.

2.6 BRIDGING THE TWO DISCIPLINES

The final section of this chapter leads into our upcoming discussion: though Astro Vedic and Vastu operate on different dimensions, when combined, they can offer deeper insights into timing and placement—two pillars of creating a successful and harmonious life.

2.7 CASE STUDIES: REAL-LIFE APPLICATIONS OF ASTRO VEDIC AND VASTU SHASTRA

CASE STUDY 1: ASTRO VEDIC – TURNING CAREER STRUGGLES INTO SUCCESS

Name: Priya Mehta

Profession: Marketing Professional

Issue: Frequent job losses and career stagnation despite qualifications and effort.

BACKGROUND:

Priya had changed jobs five times in four years. Despite her hard work and relevant skills, she constantly faced issues at the workplace—conflicts with supervisors, delayed promotions, and unstable roles. She began to doubt her capabilities.

ASTROLOGICAL INSIGHT:

After consulting a Vedic astrologer, her birth chart revealed a weak 10th house (Career House) and an ongoing Shani Dasha (Saturn period), known for testing patience and discipline. Saturn was placed in a conflicting house, causing delays and obstacles in professional growth.

REMEDIES IMPLEMENTED:

- Wore a blue sapphire ring after proper planetary verification.

- Donated black sesame seeds and iron items on Saturdays (remedies for Saturn).

- Began meditation and self-discipline practices.

- Advised to switch industries during a more favorable planetary period.

OUTCOME:

Within six months, Priya secured a stable job with a multinational firm where she was promoted within a year. More importantly, she felt mentally at peace and in control.

TAKEAWAY:

Astro Vedic did not magically change her life overnight—it gave her clarity on timing and personal tendencies, helping her take informed actions.

CASE STUDY 2: VASTU SHASTRA – RESTORING HARMONY IN A BUSINESS

Name: Gupta Family

Location: Jaipur, Rajasthan

Issue: Financial losses and constant health issues after shifting to a new home.

BACKGROUND:

The Gupta family had recently moved into a modern duplex in a posh locality. Within a few months, Mr. Gupta's business suffered major losses, and his wife began experiencing recurring illnesses. They tried medical and business consultations but saw no improvements.

VASTU ANALYSIS:

- A Vastu expert visited their home and found several imbalances:

- Main entrance was in the southwest, which is considered inauspicious.

- Kitchen was in the north, clashing with the fire element.

- The Brahmasthan (center) of the home was cluttered with heavy furniture.

CORRECTIONS APPLIED:

- Shifted the main entrance to South-Southeast.

- Relocated the kitchen to the southeast.

- Cleared the central area and added a small skylight for natural energy flow.

- Placed a mirror in the northeast corner to enhance positive energy.

OUTCOME:

In the following months, business performance improved, health stabilized, and the home atmosphere turned peaceful. The family reported better sleep, focus, and communication.

TAKEAWAY:

Minor Vastu corrections can have significant impact when made in alignment with natural energies.

CASE STUDY 3 : INTEGRATING ASTRO VEDIC AND VASTU SHASTRA FOR HOLISTIC LIFE IMPROVEMENT

Name: Arvind Kumar

Profession: Chartered Accountant

Location: Pune, Maharashtra

Issue: Stagnation in career growth, rising family tensions, and persistent health issues.

BACKGROUND:

Arvind had been running his own CA practice for over a decade. While his early career saw moderate success, in recent years his business had plateaued. At the same time, his wife began facing anxiety issues, his son struggled with academic performance, and Arvind himself developed chronic back pain. He also mentioned frequent arguments and a growing sense of negativity at home.

STEP 1: ASTRO VEDIC CONSULTATION

A detailed birth chart analysis revealed:

- **Rahu in the 4th house**: causing domestic unrest and mental instability at home.

- **Saturn Mahadasha**: a testing period known for slow progress and karmic lessons.

- **Weak Mars in the 6th house**: affecting Arvind's physical energy and willpower.

- **Remedy:** The astrologer suggested that while timing was not ideal for expansion, small corrections along with Vastu balancing could bring relief.

STEP 2: VASTU SHASTRA ANALYSIS OF HOME AND OFFICE

A certified Vastu expert visited both locations:

- Home Issues Found:
    - The bedroom was in the northwest, causing restlessness and poor sleep.
    - The main door opened to the SSW, which can attract negative energy.
    - The study room for the child was in the southwest, an area better suited for master bedrooms.

- Office Issues Found:
    - Arvind's work desk faced south, which in Vastu is considered counterproductive.

- o The cash locker was placed in the north, which is not ideal for financial flow.

CORRECTIVE MEASURES TAKEN:

- Astro Vedic Remedies:

    - o Regular chanting of Rahu beej mantra and lighting a lamp on Saturdays.

    - o Initiating new deals only on astrologically favorable days.

- Vastu Adjustments at Home:

    - o Master bedroom shifted to the southwest.

    - o Entrance shifted to SSE.

    - o Study area moved to the east, promoting concentration and calm.

- Vastu Adjustments at Office:

    - o Work desk repositioned to face north-east.

    - o Cash locker relocated to the southwest, opening towards the north.

RESULT (OVER 4 MONTHS):

- Arvind experienced a renewed sense of motivation, and his clients began returning with higher-value projects.

- Family harmony improved, with a notable decline in arguments and anxiety.

- His son began performing better academically.

- Arvind's health stabilized, with his back pain nearly gone and energy levels returning.

KEY TAKEAWAY:

When used in isolation, both Astro Vedic and Vastu Shastra are powerful tools. However, when integrated thoughtfully, they address both time-based tendencies and space-based energies, allowing for a comprehensive transformation of life conditions.

"It felt like everything just fell into place—once we stopped blaming circumstances and started aligning with nature."

— *Arvind Kumar*

CHAPTER 3: HOW ASTRO VEDIC AND VASTU SHASTRA ARE IMPORTANT IN ONE'S LIFE

3.1 UNDERSTANDING THE ROLE OF ENERGIES IN DAILY LIFE

In our modern lives, much attention is given to education, effort, and external resources as keys to success. However, countless individuals observe that despite hard work and good intentions, results often fall short. This is where the subtle sciences of **Astro Vedic and Vastu Shastra** play a vital role. Both systems emphasize the **alignment of human life with natural cosmic energies**—offering a roadmap for achieving harmony, prosperity, and peace.

Astrology (Jyotish Shastra) governs **time** and planetary influences, while Vastu Shastra governs **space** and its interaction with energy. When these two disciplines are properly understood and applied, they offer a framework for living a more synchronized life—spiritually, emotionally, and materially.

3.2 ASTRO VEDIC: THE TIMELINES OF LIFE

Astro Vedic astrology is not about predicting doomsday; it is a **scientific tool** to understand the timing of opportunities and challenges in life. Each person is born with a unique planetary configuration—called a **natal chart or horoscope**—that reflects their karmic tendencies, strengths, and vulnerabilities.

For example:

- A person undergoing **Shani Mahadasha (Saturn major period)** may experience delays, tests, and isolation—unless the energy is respected and managed through discipline and duty.

- A favorable **Jupiter transit** can open doors for education, marriage, or spiritual growth.

This **time-based guidance** allows individuals to plan better, avoid impulsive decisions, and focus their efforts during productive periods.

3.3 VASTU SHASTRA: HARMONIZING THE LIVING ENVIRONMENT

Just as astrology manages the "when," **Vastu manages the "where."** Our homes, offices, and even the land we build on are filled with vibrational energy. Vastu Shastra guides how to **design and orient spaces** to align with natural forces such as sunlight, magnetic fields, wind directions, and gravitational pull.

Examples of Vastu's impact:

- A kitchen placed in the southeast (the fire zone) improves digestion and financial well-being.

- A toilet in the northeast (the zone of clarity) can lead to confusion, poor decision-making, and even financial drains and Severe Health Issues.

Correct Vastu alignment can enhance health, mental peace, and success, while incorrect placement can amplify stress and obstacles, regardless of how modern or luxurious a building may appear.

3.4 THE COMBINED EFFECT: TIME AND SPACE IN BALANCE

While Vedic Astrology tells us **what energies are influencing our life and when**, Vastu tells us **how to manage the space we inhabit** to either amplify or neutralize those influences.

EXAMPLE SCENARIO:

A person's chart may show a weak Mars, indicating low confidence and delayed decision-making. If the same person's home has a cluttered southeast corner (associated with Mars and fire), the problem worsens. Cleaning and activating that space with Vastu principles can help balance that planetary deficiency.

Thus, together they form a holistic diagnostic and healing system.

3.5 MENTAL HEALTH AND ENERGY FLOW

One of the most **underrated aspects** of both sciences is their effect on mental health. Many modern problems—insomnia, anxiety, restlessness, or even depression—have been linked to disharmonious living spaces or unfavorable astrological periods.

- Vastu can address mental fatigue by enhancing light and energy flow in specific zones.

- Astro Vedic remedies can provide emotional stability and resilience during tough planetary periods.

Rather than replacing medicine or therapy, they act as **complementary aids** for holistic well-being.

3.6 SUPPORTING SPIRITUAL AND MATERIAL GROWTH

In a balanced approach, these sciences do not reject material life. Instead, they support both **material success and spiritual growth**:

- Astro Vedic helps us understand the **karmic lessons** we are meant to learn.

- Vastu ensures our external environment supports our internal journey.

Together, they create a strong foundation for living with clarity, purpose, and success.

3.7 Conclusion: The Science of Alignment

Astro Vedic and Vastu Shastra are not about superstition or blind belief. They are tools to **optimize life through awareness and alignment**. Just as one consults a doctor or architect for specialized insight, these sciences provide deeper understanding of life's invisible patterns. When used wisely, they transform uncertainty into clarity and chaos into harmony.

EXAMPLE 1: A CAREER NOT TAKING OFF DESPITE TALENT

BACKGROUND:

Sneha, a talented graphic designer, faced repeated job losses and conflicts with managers despite positive feedback about her work.

ASTRO VEDIC INSIGHT:

Her chart showed a debilitated Sun and ongoing Rahu period — leading to lack of recognition and authority issues.

VASTU INSIGHT:

Her home's **northeast zone (zone of clarity and blessings)** was cluttered with unused furniture and leaking pipes, and her **work desk faced a blank wall.**

CORRECTIVE ACTIONS:

- Activated northeast with natural light, yellow decor, and a water bowl.

- Rearranged her desk to face east (direction of growth).

- Chanted the **Aditya Hridayam** daily to strengthen the Sun.

RESULT:

Within two months, Sneha was hired by a reputed design firm and promoted within the first year.

EXAMPLE 2: CHILD'S LEARNING AND CONCENTRATION ISSUES

BACKGROUND:

A 12-year-old boy struggled with memory, poor concentration, and reluctance to study.

ASTRO VEDIC INSIGHT:

His Mercury was weak and afflicted by Ketu—hindering communication and learning ability.

VASTU INSIGHT:

His study area was in the **southwest**, the zone of stability, but also a place better suited for adults.

CORRECTIVE ACTIONS:

- Moved his study table to the **northeast** (the zone of wisdom).

- Encouraged early morning sunlight exposure.

- Gave him a green crystal on his desk and performed simple Mercury-related chanting.

RESULT:

The child began to enjoy studies and his academic performance improved steadily over 6 months.

EXAMPLE 3: CONSTANT HEALTH PROBLEMS IN THE FAMILY

BACKGROUND:

A family of four was facing recurring health issues—mostly digestive and respiratory.

ASTRO VEDIC INSIGHT:

Multiple family members were under the influence of Ketu or Shani (Saturn) transits, known for chronic health issues.

VASTU INSIGHT:

- Kitchen was in the **north**, which is water-dominated and unsuitable for fire (Agni).

- Southeast (fire zone) was used as a toilet.

CORRECTIVE ACTIONS:

- Converted the north kitchen into a store room and moved cooking to southeast.

- Used copper vessels and energizing Agni yantras.

- Introduced herbal remedies based on planetary energies.

RESULT:

The family reported significantly fewer illnesses and improved digestion within 3–4 months.

EXAMPLE 4: FINANCIAL LOSSES IN BUSINESS

BACKGROUND:

Ramesh, a boutique owner, saw declining sales and rising debts even during festive seasons.

ASTRO VEDIC INSIGHT:

Saturn was transiting his 8th house (career), and Mars was weak in his birth chart—affecting decision-making and drive.

VASTU INSIGHT:

- The **cash counter faced the entrance**, a poor placement for wealth retention.

- The **southwest corner** had a broken mirror and open shelves—causing leakage of money.

CORRECTIVE ACTIONS:

- Moved the cash counter to **southwest**, facing north.

- Fixed broken mirrors, cleaned up open shelves, and placed a solid heavy safe with Gomti chakra inside.

- Shani Chaya Patra Daan

- Chanting Mantra 108times Daily – "Om Vasudevaya Namah"

- Perform Laxmi Puja with lotus flower.

- Energised North with water element and Southeast with fire element.

RESULT:

Sales gradually recovered, and he was able to clear a major portion of his debt within a year.

CONCLUSION OF EXAMPLES SECTION

These examples show that **Astro Vedic timing (what and when)** and **Vastu Shastra positioning (where and how)** complement each other like two parts of a complete formula. By correcting both the **time-based karma** and **space-based energy**, individuals can experience visible, positive transformations in all areas of life.

CHAPTER 4: HOW THE VASTU OF LAND MATTERS

INTRODUCTION

In Vastu Shastra, the land is not just a physical foundation—it is the energetic base of all future developments. The orientation, slope, shape, and energy flow of land influence every aspect of life, from health and wealth to peace of mind and relationships. With the evolution of traditional Vastu, Vishal Agarwal's approach uses the **16-direction method**, allowing for **greater precision** in diagnosis and remedies.

THE SCIENCE BEHIND LAND ENERGY

Land acts as a **receptor of cosmic energy**, and its interaction with natural elements (earth, water, fire, air, and space) creates a **vibrational environment**. Every corner, edge, and direction corresponds to a specific **planetary influence**, element, and life aspect.

In the **16-direction system**, each direction—cardinal, intercardinal, and sub-cardinal—has a distinct significance. For instance:

Direction	Associated Planet	Life Aspect
East	Sun	Name, fame, new beginnings, Socialization
West	Saturn	Stability, maturity, Profits and Wish fulfilment
North	Mercury	Finance, intelligence, Opportunity and Direction
South	Mars	Strength, courage, Stability
NE (Ishan)	Jupiter	Wisdom, clarity, blessings
SE (Agneya)	Venus	Fire, health, energy, Money
NW (Vayavya)	Moon	Emotions, networking, Support, Banking
SW (Nairutya)	Rahu	Ancestors, stability, control
ENE	Sun & Jupiter	Leadership, spiritual growth, Happiness, Humour and Hobbies
ESE	Venus & Sun	Vitality, beauty, Churning and clarity
SSE	Mars & Venus	Physical health, aggression, Confidence and popularity
SSW	Mars & Rahu	Accidents, legal issues, Expenditure
WSW	Saturn & Rahu	Delays, karmic lessons, Savings, Education
WNW	Saturn & Moon	Trust, mental pressure, Depression, Tension
NNW	Mercury & Moon	Creativity, communication, Couple-Relationship, Attractiveness

NNE	Mercury & Jupiter	Wealth through intellect, Health, Medical Recovery

KEY ELEMENTS IN EVALUATING LAND

- **Shape of the Land**

  o **Square or rectangular plots** (with equal or near-equal dimensions) are most auspicious.

  o Irregular shapes often create directional imbalances, which reflect in life issues like instability or stagnation.

- **Slope and Elevation**

  o **North-East lower and South-West higher** is ideal: encourages divine inflow of energy.

  o Opposite gradients (e.g., NE higher, SW lower) can reverse fortune and create struggles.

- **Road Facing**

  o Each facing (e.g., North-East corner plot, East-facing, West-facing) has different effects based on the activities planned on that land.

- **Obstructions and Openings**

  o Trees, electric poles, or open drains in certain directions (especially NE or ESE) can block or corrupt beneficial energies.

  o Wide, clean NE and NNW openings welcome prosperity and mental peace.

IMPACT OF BAD VASTU IN PROPERTY SELECTION

Ignoring land Vastu often leads to **unexplainable difficulties**, such as:

- **Financial instability** despite hard work.

- **Family disputes** in otherwise harmonious households.

- **Health problems** that recur or don't respond to treatment.

- **Business losses** from good ventures.

These outcomes are often the result of:

- Major directional defects (e.g., toilets in NE or kitchens in NW),

- Living or working in zones governed by conflicting energies,

- Poorly balanced energy flow due to external surroundings.

CASE STUDY: PLOT SELECTION FOR A WELLNESS CENTRE

SCENARIO:

A client wished to build a wellness retreat center in Assam. A lush, spacious land parcel was selected, but the client faced repeated rejections from architects and licensing authorities.

VASTU & ASTRO VEDIC ASSESSMENT (16-DIRECTION):

The **SSW (South-Southwest)** had a large pond — water element in a fire-dominated zone.

The **ENE (East-Northeast)** had tall eucalyptus trees blocking the morning sun (Sun-Jupiter energy blocked).

The client was undergoing a **Saturn major period**, indicating karmic delays when aligned with wrong energy zones.

REMEDY & OUTCOME:

The pond was relocated to the **North zone** and a Tulsi mandap built in ENE.

North to east area was dedicated to Open space, Pond, Gardening and sitting spaces.

Energy balancing using copper pyramids in SSW.

Client performed Saturn remedies (Shani chant, oil lamp in iron bowl every Saturday).

The project was greenlit in 6 weeks and completed successfully.

BENEFITS OF FOLLOWING LAND VASTU (16-DIRECTION METHOD)

- Enhanced **clarity and focus** for the inhabitants.
- Improved **health and immunity**.
- Better **financial prospects and cash flow**.
- Stronger **relationships and emotional balance**.
- A feeling of **peace and alignment** with nature's laws.

CONCLUSION

The land we choose to live or work on is not just a piece of real estate—it is a **living energy field**. The 16-direction approach gives us an edge in precisely mapping these fields and **tuning them to cosmic harmony**. By evaluating and balancing the land through this expanded lens, one can pave the way for **success, health, and spiritual growth**.

CHAPTER 5: WHY ONE NEEDS TO CHECK THE VASTU

INTRODUCTION

Vastu Shastra is not merely a set of ancient beliefs or customs—it is a **systematic architectural science** rooted in spatial energy, cosmic alignment, and planetary influence. The necessity of checking Vastu before occupying or constructing a space arises from the fact that every **physical space interacts with human psychology and destiny**. The 16-direction method followed by Vishal Agarwal offers **deeper diagnostic accuracy**, making Vastu analysis not just relevant but essential in modern life.

VASTU AS AN ENERGETIC BLUEPRINT

Each structure has an **energy blueprint**, much like a human being has a DNA code. This energetic pattern is formed through:

- The **orientation of the plot or building**.

- The **functional usage of each zone** (e.g., kitchen, toilet, prayer room).

- The **distribution of elements** (fire, water, air, earth, space).

- The **directional balance** based on the 16-zone grid.

When these aspects are misaligned, the result is **energetic disharmony**—which manifests as real-life struggles. Hence, **checking Vastu is akin to checking the pulse of your environment**.

WHEN TO CHECK THE VASTU

- **Before Buying Land or Property**

    o Prevents investment in zones that carry negative karmic imprints or directional faults.

    o Ensures that the property's energy supports the buyer's **astrological chart**.

- **Before Starting Construction**

    o Identifies ideal placements of rooms and utilities based on the directional grid.

    o Avoids irreversible design flaws.

- **Before Moving In**

    o Allows for necessary corrections or energy balancing (even without structural changes).

    o Sets the tone for a peaceful, successful life in that space.

- **During Life's Major Transitions**

    o Marriage, childbirth, new business, or career shifts: these require energetic alignment for smooth progress.

16-DIRECTION ZONES AND THEIR RELEVANCE

Each of the 16 directions governs a **specific aspect of life**. Here's why checking them is crucial:

Direction	Importance of Vastu Check
NE (Ishan)	Clarity of mind, divine connection – sensitive to water/toilet defects.
SE (Agneya)	Health, digestion – critical for placing kitchen or fire zones.
SW (Nairutya)	Stability, ancestral blessings – imbalances can cause anxiety, instability.

Even a **small deviation in one direction**—like placing a septic tank in ENE—can disturb the cosmic energy matrix.

CASE STUDY: RESIDENTIAL FLAT IN A METRO CITY

BACKGROUND:

A family in Mumbai moved into a 3BHK apartment on the 7th floor. Within 3 months, they noticed rising tension between parents and children, frequent illnesses, and job stagnation.

VASTU ANALYSIS (16-DIRECTION):

- The **kitchen was located in the NW,** which is ruled by the Moon – fire in a water-emotion zone.

- The **toilet was placed in NNE,** disrupting finance and career progress.

- The **main door was in WSW,** associated with karmic burdens and delays.

REMEDIAL MEASURES:

- Installed copper strips under kitchen slab to neutralize fire–water clash.

- Vastu salt and brass pyramids placed in NNE toilet.

- Activated North and ENE zones using green plants and Jupiter yantra.

OUTCOME:

Improved family harmony, father got a promotion, and child recovered from recurring health issues.

COMMON SIGNS OF VASTU IMBALANCE

- Constant **financial leaks** despite adequate income.

- Repetitive **health issues** with no medical diagnosis.

- **Mental stress**, anxiety, or sleep disturbances.

- **Stuck projects,** delays in approvals, or failing business launches.

- Disrupted **relationships or family dynamics**.

These are all red flags to check the Vastu energy grid—especially via the **expanded 16-direction model**.

MODERN RELEVANCE OF VASTU CHECKING

In today's world of high-rises, shared walls, and tech-filled homes, many people assume Vastu doesn't apply. On the contrary:

- Vastu **adapts to all building types**—apartments, duplexes, offices, shops.

- The 16-direction grid allows for **micro-analysis**, even in compact urban spaces.

- **Non-invasive remedies** (colors, metal strips, symbols) enable corrections without renovation.

Even corporate entities now use Vastu audits to realign their **headquarters and boardrooms** to zones of growth, networking, and clear communication.

CONCLUSION

Checking the Vastu of a space is not a superstition—it is an act of **proactive energy alignment**. The expanded 16-direction method practiced by Vishal Agarwal allows individuals and families to make **informed decisions** about where and how they live, work, and grow. In a world full of chaos and uncertainty, **a Vastu-aligned environment becomes a stable anchor** to support and uplift human potential.

CHAPTER 6: HOW VASTU SHASTRA AND ASTRO VEDIC ARE DIFFERENT BUT WORK TOGETHER

INTRODUCTION

Vastu Shastra and Astro Vedic (Vedic Astrology) are **two distinct yet complementary systems** rooted in the same ancient Indian wisdom. While one focuses on the **external environment**, the other reveals the **internal cosmic blueprint** of an individual. Understanding the **difference between them** and how they **interact synergistically** is crucial for holistic living and future planning. Vishal Agarwal's unique approach leverages both sciences—especially through the **16-direction method**—to provide **customized, practical solutions**.

FUNDAMENTAL DIFFERENCE

Aspect	Vastu Shastra	Astro Vedic (Jyotish Shastra)
Focus	Space, directions, architecture	Time, planetary positions, birth chart
Subject of Study	Land, buildings, physical environment	Human life, karma, destiny

Nature	Static (external layout)	Dynamic (based on time and transit)
Tools Used	16-direction grid, elemental zones	Horoscope (kundali), dasha system, planetary charts
Applications	Home, offices, temples, public spaces	Career, marriage, health, finance, spirituality

Though different in function, both are interdependent forces. Just as the human body and environment constantly interact, so do these sciences.

HOW THEY WORK TOGETHER

1. ALIGNING THE CHART WITH THE SPACE

Astro Vedic provides the **blueprint of a person's life** through their natal chart (Janma Kundali). This helps identify:

- Strong and weak planets

- Favorable and unfavorable directions

- Ongoing planetary periods (Mahadasha)

Vastu Shastra uses this information to **tailor the energy flow** of a space, enhancing planetary support. For example:

- A person ruled by **Mars** (fire element) may benefit from a **SSE(S3, S4) Entry**

- A native under **Saturn's dasha** may require boosting the **WSW zone** for karmic release.

2. CORRECTING DESTINY THROUGH SPACE

While astrology highlights **what is destined**, Vastu offers **a way to correct or minimize suffering** by modifying the energy in one's surroundings.

Example:

If someone is facing repeated delays in marriage due to **Venus or Moon afflictions**, Vastu corrections in **NW (relationships)** and **NNE (mental balance)** can create shifts, leading to smoother outcomes.

3. TIMING VASTU CHANGES WITH ASTROLOGY

Even the **timing of Vastu changes**—like housewarming, shifting homes, or activating a zone—can be chosen based on **planetary transits** or favorable muhurats from Vedic Astrology.

This synchronization ensures that the correction is **cosmically supported**, creating faster and more harmonious results.

CASE STUDY: A BUSINESSMAN'S RISE WITH BOTH SCIENCES

Client: Mr. S, 42, textile exporter from Ahmedabad.

Issue: Business stagnation, Less overseas orders for 18 months.

ASTROLOGICAL INSIGHTS:

- Mercury was in a weak house in his lagna Chart.

- Rahu positioned in 8th house – creating confusion and delays.

VASTU OBSERVATIONS (16-DIRECTION):

- The **ENE zone (creativity, marketing)** had a store room filled with clutter.

- **SSE (cash flow)** had a toilet, draining financial energy.

- **NNW (communication)** was blocked due to a staircase.

SOLUTIONS:

- Cleared ENE and added green element + Mercury yantra.

- Converted toilet use to storage and applied brass Vastu strips in SSE.

- Activated with mirrors and lights to finished goods display area in NNW

- Activated North with Kuber Yantra and a fountain.

RESULT:

Within 3 months, received a bulk order from Europe, followed by steady overseas growth.

REAL-WORLD PARALLEL

Think of Vastu as the **hardware** and Astrology as the **software**.

- Hardware without software: The space is ready but lacks life direction.

- Software without hardware: Strong potential, but the environment blocks or delays expression.

Only when **both align**, the system works efficiently.

16-DIRECTION MODEL: THE BRIDGE

Vishal's model uses **both sciences to map out human life's zones**:

- Career: NNE, ENE + aligned with 10th house in astrology

- Health: SSE, ESE + 6th house

- Marriage: NW, NNW + 7th house

- Finance: SW, WSW + 2nd/11th house

- Spirituality: NE, NNE + 12th/9th house

This integrated method ensures **not just prediction but transformation**.

CONCLUSION

While Vastu and Astro Vedic may seem like parallel tracks, they're actually two wheels of the same chariot. Vastu helps **stabilize and direct** the energies revealed by Astrology. When used together, they offer **a complete toolkit to shape one's destiny**—scientifically, logically, and spiritually.

CHAPTER 7: THE IMPORTANCE OF THE LAND'S VASTU IN SHAPING YOUR FUTURE

INTRODUCTION

The land you choose to build on or live in is not just a physical space; it is **an energetic entity** that profoundly influences the lives of those who inhabit it. Just as your own birth chart governs your life's course, the **Vastu of the land** governs the flow of energy in and around your living or working space. Understanding the **Vastu of the land** is not just about improving aesthetics or comfort; it is about optimizing the space to align with **your life's energy**, goals, and destiny.

In this chapter, we will explore how the **Vastu of the land** impacts the future of the people who inhabit it, and why it's important to check this fundamental aspect before construction or purchase. Vishal Agarwal's **16-direction method** takes into account these subtle energetic influences, offering a more detailed understanding of land's Vastu and how to harness its power effectively.

THE COSMIC CONNECTION BETWEEN LAND AND DESTINY

Land, like humans, carries **inherent energies** influenced by multiple factors, such as:

- **Geological structure** (e.g., hills, rivers, underground water).

- **Cosmic influences** (planets, stars, and constellations at the time of construction).

- **Human influence** (previous owners, historical significance).

Just as your astrological chart maps your life's journey, the **Vastu of the land** plays a pivotal role in shaping the opportunities, health, and prosperity you experience.

Example:

If the plot is in a **seismic zone**, the land itself may be unstable. If it is near a river that carries **negative energy**, there may be disruptions in prosperity and peace. Such factors should be evaluated before making any decisions.

HOW VASTU OF THE LAND AFFECTS DIFFERENT ASPECTS OF LIFE

1. HEALTH AND WELL-BEING

The land's **subsurface energy** plays a significant role in physical health. For example:

- If the **land has underground water veins**, the electromagnetic field can cause disruptions in the body's **bio-energy**, leading to sleep disturbances, fatigue, or chronic illnesses.

- The **topography of the land,** such as **elevations and depressions**, impacts the flow of vital energy (Prana). Land that is **higher on the south side and lower on the north** is typically more beneficial as it aligns with natural energy flows.

2. FINANCIAL PROSPERITY AND SUCCESS

A **balanced plot** with no imbalance in elements (fire, water, air, earth) attracts positive energy, leading to **financial growth**. Conversely:

- **Sloping land towards the north or east** (direction of wealth and prosperity) brings in **good fortune**.

- **Land sloping towards the south** may lead to **financial instability** and stagnation, as it disrupts the natural flow of positive energy.

3. CAREER AND GROWTH

The **Vastu of the land** also governs the **energy flow in business and career sectors**. For instance:

- A **southern or southwestern plot** can be conducive to **stability and leadership** roles, suitable for owners or executives of a company.

- An **eastern or northeastern plot** can enhance **creative energy**, attracting **opportunities** for growth in arts, media, or technology.

4. RELATIONSHIPS AND HARMONY

The **relationship energy** of a space is greatly affected by the land's orientation and usage:

- The **north-western zone (Vayavya)** governs **communication** and **relationships**. A plot that is **open and free of obstructions in this zone** fosters open communication and harmonious relations.

- A **toilet or heavy machinery** in the **NW** can create disturbances in **personal and professional relationships**, leading to constant misunderstandings and conflicts.

CASE STUDY: THE POWER OF LAND VASTU IN REAL ESTATE

Client: Ms. R, 34, a real estate investor from Pune.

Issue: Ms. R purchased a plot in the western region of the city to build a commercial property. Despite great location and investment potential, her business faced constant delays, disputes with contractors, and customer dissatisfaction.

Land Vastu Analysis (16-Direction):

- **South-West slope**: The land sloped downward toward the south, causing imbalance and **negative energy accumulation** in the property.

- **Underground water flow**: Hidden water veins were found in the northeast, leading to **health-related problems** for her construction workers.

Solutions:

- Introduced **copper rods** and **yantras** to neutralize the water flow.

- Adjusted the **topography** by leveling the south-western section and created a **high point in the north** to realign the energy.

Outcome:

Once corrected, Ms. R's business flourished. The contractors began working without delays, and customer satisfaction rose, leading to high returns on her investment.

THE ROLE OF THE 16-DIRECTION METHOD IN LAND VASTU

Vishal Agarwal's 16-direction method provides a **detailed and comprehensive approach** to land Vastu, considering each zone's influence on various life aspects. The precision of this method allows one to **map out all significant areas** in the land, whether it is for personal, residential, or commercial use.

- **Zones for Health (SW, SE, NNE)**: Identifying and fixing areas that might disrupt physical or mental health.

- **Zones for Prosperity (NE, N, ENE)**: Ensuring that the plot attracts financial growth and career success.

- **Zones for Relationships (NW, NNW)**: Activating the energy fields that promote peaceful relationships and open communication.

CHOOSING LAND BASED ON VASTU

1. CHECKING THE DIRECTION OF THE PLOT

- A plot facing the **East** is usually ideal for **spiritual development, wealth, and communication**.

- A **South-facing plot** requires more **careful alignment** due to the potential dominance of **negative energy**. However, with the right Vastu corrections, it can be balanced for prosperity.

2. ASSESSING THE SHAPE OF THE LAND

- **Rectangular or square plots** are considered the most **balanced**.

- **Irregular plots**, especially those with cut corners or shapes that are not symmetrical, tend to create **instability** and disharmony in the space.

3. NATURAL FEATURES

- **Trees**, especially those with strong roots or **water sources**, should be placed correctly. For instance, **a large tree** in the **NW** can lead to **stagnation in relationships and communication**.

CONCLUSION

In the complex dance between **space and energy**, the **Vastu of the land** plays a crucial role in determining the **success or failure** of any venture, whether it's personal, professional, or financial. By aligning with the energies of the **16-direction grid**, individuals can ensure that the **land they inhabit or invest in** supports their life's goals.

Incorporating **land Vastu checks** before purchase or construction can save time, energy, and investment by preemptively aligning the environment with one's **destiny**.

Vishal Agarwal's **16-direction method** allows for **detailed diagnostics** that help bring out the **best in any plot**, creating a harmonious, prosperous, and successful life for its inhabitants.

CHAPTER 8: ALIGNING ASTRO VEDIC WITH VASTU SHASTRA FOR A HARMONIOUS LIFE

INTRODUCTION

Vastu Shastra and Astro Vedic, when combined, create a potent synergy that can transform your life in profound ways. While each discipline stands strong on its own, **Astro Vedic** offers insights from **astrology** that complement the physical alignment of spaces dictated by **Vastu Shastra**. This chapter explores how these two ancient sciences work together and how you can align both to achieve a **harmonious and prosperous life**.

Incorporating both elements helps bridge the **cosmic and earthly realms**, providing a **holistic approach to living**. While Vastu Shastra works on the foundation of your physical surroundings, Astro Vedic deals with the **planets, stars**, and **astrological influences**. Together, they provide a **comprehensive solution** for enhancing personal growth, relationships, career success, and overall well-being.

UNDERSTANDING THE INTEGRATION OF ASTRO VEDIC AND VASTU SHASTRA

WHAT IS ASTRO VEDIC?

Astro Vedic is the application of **Vedic astrology** in the practice of **Vastu Shastra**. While Vastu focuses on the **physical energies** in a space, Astro Vedic draws on the influence of **celestial bodies** (like planets, stars, and the moon) on your life. It looks at your **birth chart** and assesses how the alignment of celestial bodies impacts your day-to-day life and your interactions with your surroundings.

Vishal Agarwal's **16-direction method** integrates this by not just focusing on the physical aspects of the land and property, but also considering the **astrological aspects** related to each direction.

ASTRO VEDIC AND VASTU IN SYNC

When **Astro Vedic** is applied in conjunction with **Vastu Shastra**, the individual's **birth chart** and **planetary positions** are considered when designing the home or workspace. The goal is to align **planetary energies** with the physical environment, ensuring that there is a **flow of positive energy** that nurtures the person's **personal, professional, and spiritual growth**.

For example:

- If someone's **birth chart** shows a strong influence of **Mars** (a planet that governs action, strength, and energy), their home or office should be oriented in such a way that it taps into the **south** or **southwest** directions, aligning the planetary influences with the space.

- Conversely, a **Venus**-influenced person (governing beauty, love, and harmony) would benefit from spaces aligned with **the northeast or the east**.

By taking both **Vastu** and **Astro Vedic** into account, we can design a space that doesn't just work physically but also enhances the individual's **life journey**.

HOW ASTRO VEDIC INFLUENCES VASTU SHASTRA'S SPACE DESIGN

1. PERSONALIZED LAYOUT BASED ON BIRTH CHART

Every individual has a **unique birth chart** that tells the story of their **life path** and **destiny**. By analyzing a person's **astrological chart**, we can identify the **most favorable directions** for certain activities and **align the house or office layout** accordingly.

For instance:

- A person born under the **sign of Aries** may have a strong connection to the **south** zone, which is associated with **fire** energy. This can be ideal for areas in the house related to **activity, energy**, and **ambition**, such as the **living room** or **work space**.

- A person born under the **sign of Taurus**, which is ruled by **Venus,** would benefit from a home that incorporates the **northeast direction** for their **bedroom** or **meditation space**, as Venus governs beauty, love, and serenity.

2. CHOOSING THE RIGHT ELEMENTS FOR EACH DIRECTION

Each direction governs specific **elements** in Vastu and also has a unique astrological influence. For example:

- **North (Water Element)**: Favorable for **wealth** and **prosperity**. People with strong **Mercury** or **Jupiter** influences may benefit from placing **water features** like a **fountain** or **aquarium** in this zone.

- **South (Fire Element)**: Ideal for people with **strong Mars** or **Sun** placements. This zone should be designed with **bold** colors (like red or orange) and **activity-based** spaces like **kitchens, workspaces,** or **gyms.**

- **East (Air Element):** Great for individuals with **Moon** or **Venus** in their charts, this zone fosters **creativity, communication,** and **spiritual growth.** The placement of **windows, doors,** or **creative workspaces** in the east can help individuals capitalize on these energies.

3. INCORPORATING ASTRO VEDIC PRINCIPLES IN DAILY LIVING

Astro Vedic principles can also extend beyond physical space design to **everyday practices.** For instance, if your astrological chart suggests **weak energy in the south-east (fire zone),** it may indicate challenges in **health** or **finance.** In such cases:

- **Lighting** a lamp (or **diya**) in this zone could help balance the **fire element.**

- **Using red or yellow colors** for decor in this area could amplify energy and balance out the **negative influences** of the fire element.

CASE STUDY: ALIGNING ASTRO VEDIC WITH VASTU SHASTRA FOR ENHANCED PROSPERITY

Client: Mr. S, 42, a businessman based in Kolkata.

Issue: Mr. S was struggling with **business losses,** despite being in an ideal location for his industry. His investments were not yielding expected returns, and his personal life was also facing constant challenges.

Analysis:

- Mr. S's **birth chart** revealed strong **Saturn** influence, especially in the **northeast** (the zone of wisdom and growth).

- However, his office layout had the **main entrance in the southwest,** a zone dominated by **heavy energy** (Southwest being the zone of stability and earth).

Solution:

- Moved the office entrance towards the **northeast** and incorporated **wooden elements** and **water features** to balance his **Saturn** energy.

- Reoriented his **workstations** and **conference rooms** to **align with Jupiter's** expansive energy, fostering growth and prosperity.

Outcome:

After these adjustments, Mr. S saw a significant improvement in his business operations, with the company turning profitable within the next few months. His personal life also became more harmonious, with a better work-life balance.

CONCLUSION

Incorporating both **Astro Vedic** and **Vastu Shastra** into your life creates a **complete and harmonious alignment** between the **cosmic energies** and your **earthly surroundings.** By understanding your **personal astrological influences** and combining them with **physical space design,** you can optimize your environment to support your journey towards **success, health,** and **spiritual growth.**

By using Vishal Agarwal's **16-direction method,** one can not only align physical spaces but also draw on the **power of planetary energies** to create an environment that works in harmony with your **astrological strengths** and **challenges**. It's a comprehensive approach to achieving a life that flows effortlessly with the natural laws of the universe.

CHAPTER 9: THE ROLE OF VASTU IN ENHANCING CAREER AND WEALTH

INTRODUCTION

A significant aspect of Vastu Shastra is its potential to impact various facets of life, including **career** and **wealth**. The layout and design of your living or working space influence the flow of energy, which can either facilitate or hinder your professional success and financial prosperity.

This chapter focuses on the **importance of Vastu** in **boosting your career** and attracting **abundance**. By understanding and applying the right principles of Vastu, along with the astrological insights from **Astro Vedic**, you can create a space that not only nurtures your ambitions but also aligns with the cosmic forces to bring **success** and **financial growth**.

UNDERSTANDING VASTU AND CAREER GROWTH

1. THE POWER OF DIRECTION

Vastu Shastra associates specific directions with various aspects of **life**, including career and wealth. When your work or home space is aligned with the right energy zones, you naturally experience **growth**, **prosperity**, and **success** in those areas of life.

CAREER-RELATED DIRECTIONS

- **North** (Water Element) – Governed by **Mercury**, this direction is directly associated with **career success** and **prosperity**. People seeking to elevate their professional standing or expand their businesses should ensure that their **office** or **work space** faces the **north**. The **north zone** is also linked with **communication** and **learning**, making it ideal for those in education, media, or communication industries.

- **East** (Air Element) – Governed by the **Sun**, this direction symbolizes **new beginnings** and **growth**. If you're looking to make a **career change** or **take on a new project**, this is the direction to focus on. Ensure your **main door** or **workspace** has good **lighting** and **windows** that open to the east.

- **Southwest** (Earth Element) – This direction is linked with **stability** and **authority**. For those seeking **leadership roles** or **business stability**, the **southwest** direction helps provide the solid foundation necessary for **authority** and **control** in the workplace.

- **Southeast** (Fire Element) – While this direction is associated with **energy** and **action**, it also governs **financial stability**. Those looking to boost **wealth** or **financial investments** should focus on creating an active **financial zone** in the **southeast** of their home or office.

ASTRO VEDIC CONNECTION:

- **Saturn**, often linked with hard work, patience, and discipline, plays a major role in the **west direction**. People under **Saturn's influence** may benefit from activities related to **international business** or **travel**, making it ideal for a **global career** focus, if his astro charts allows the same.

- **Jupiter**, the planet of wisdom and expansion, governs the **northeast direction**, which is connected with **education** and

spiritual growth. Professionals in research, academia, or any form of **teaching** may benefit from placing their **workstations** or **study areas** in this direction to draw on **Jupiter's expansive energy**.

2. VASTU REMEDIES FOR CAREER PROGRESSION

While Vastu Shastra emphasizes aligning physical spaces with cosmic energies, it also offers **remedies** for those facing obstacles in their careers or financial pursuits. Here are some **simple Vastu remedies** that can be implemented to enhance career success:

REMEDIES FOR CAREER ADVANCEMENT:

- **Clear Clutter**: Vastu emphasizes the importance of a **clutter-free** and organized space. A **disorganized workspace** can hinder the flow of **positive energy** and create a sense of chaos. Keeping your workspace tidy and free from clutter allows the free movement of energy, which in turn promotes **clarity of thought** and **productivity**.

- **Use of Colors**: Colors have a significant impact on the energy of the space. If you're seeking career advancement:

  - **Blue and green** can be used in the **north** to enhance communication and intellectual skills.

  - **Yellow** and **gold** in the **east** can help boost **growth** and **learning**.

  - **Red** and **orange** can be placed in the **south** to boost **energy** and **action** in your career.

- **Proper Placement of Furniture**: Ensure that the **desk** or **work station** faces either **east** or **north** for better career outcomes. Your **desk should not face a wall**, as it can limit opportunities and block success.

- **Display of Symbols**: Certain symbols such as the **Auspicious Swastika**, **lord Ganesha**, or **a tree of life** can attract positive energies, especially in career-related zones like the **north** or **east** of the space.

- **Mirrors**: Mirrors in the **north** can reflect **prosperity** and **expand opportunities**. However, avoid placing mirrors in the **southwest** or **south**, as they can disrupt **stability**.

CASE STUDY: BOOSTING CAREER SUCCESS WITH VASTU

Client: Mrs. R, 36, a senior manager at a multinational company.

Issue: Despite her expertise, Mrs. R felt **stagnation** in her career. She faced frequent **obstacles** in getting promotions, and her financial growth was slower than expected.

ANALYSIS:

Mrs. R's **office** was located in the **southwest** corner of the building, which is generally associated with **stability** but also can restrict **growth** and **expansion**.

Her desk was placed in a **corner** with **poor lighting**, and she lacked **clear visibility** of her **career opportunities**.

SOLUTION:

We recommended moving her desk towards the **north zone** of the office, aligning it with **Mercury's** energy for improved **communication** and **career advancement**.

We also suggested the addition of a **small plant** to the **northeast** of her desk, enhancing **growth** and **prosperity**.

The office entrance was shifted to face the **east**, promoting **new beginnings** and **positive energy** for her career.

OUTCOME:

Within a few months of applying these Vastu remedies, Mrs. R was promoted to a **higher management role**. She also reported a **significant improvement in her financial situation** and a more harmonious work environment.

CONCLUSION

Vastu Shastra offers a powerful and effective way to influence your career and wealth by creating spaces that attract positive energy. When you align your living or work environment with the **right energies**, both physical and celestial, you open doors to **growth, prosperity**, and **success**.

By integrating Astro Vedic insights into Vastu practices, you can create a space that not only **nurtures your career** but also attracts **financial abundance** and **overall well-being**. This holistic approach helps to **balance** both the **physical** and **cosmic energies**, ensuring a smooth and prosperous journey toward success.

CHAPTER 10: VASTU AND HEALTH: CREATING A HARMONIOUS ENVIRONMENT FOR WELL-BEING

INTRODUCTION

The impact of Vastu Shastra extends beyond just career and financial growth; it plays a vital role in shaping your **physical, emotional, and mental health**. A harmonious environment according to Vastu principles can significantly improve your overall well-being, reduce stress, and promote health and vitality. This chapter explores how aligning your living space with the natural elements can enhance your health, help in disease prevention, and create a peaceful, balanced environment conducive to good health.

VASTU AND HEALTH: UNDERSTANDING THE CONNECTION

1. THE ROLE OF DIRECTIONS IN HEALTH

Vastu Shastra associates different **directions** with specific elements of life. When it comes to health, these directions influence the **energy flow** and the balance of the **five elements** (Earth, Water, Fire, Air, and Space) in your home. The correct alignment of these elements can enhance overall well-being.

KEY DIRECTIONS FOR HEALTH:

- **North-East (Water & Space)** – The North-East direction is the most important zone for health, as it governs mental clarity, spirituality, and overall well-being. A clutter-free, clean, and well-lit space in the north-east helps promote health and encourages a calm, peaceful atmosphere. If your bedroom or living area is located here, it can create a balanced and positive energy flow.

- **North**-NorthEast – This Direction is for Immunity and Medical Recovery.

- **East (Air & Sun)** – The East is associated with new beginnings, vitality, and energy. Sunlight plays an essential role in boosting physical health, and exposure to morning sunlight can be revitalizing for the body and mind. Keeping windows or open spaces on the east side allows the fresh air and sunlight to enter, creating an energetic and healthy environment.

- **South-East (Fire)** – The South-East governs the digestive system and overall metabolism. This direction is linked to the Fire element, and ensuring that this zone remains vibrant and energized helps in balancing the body's metabolic processes. Too much clutter or a dark, stagnant South-East can lead to digestive problems, irritability, and a general lack of vitality.

- **South-West (Earth)** – This direction governs stability and grounding, which are necessary for maintaining both physical and emotional health. A heavy presence of furniture in the southwest can provide physical strength and promote a sense of security. However, it is essential not to over-clutter this zone as it could result in a sense of being overwhelmed and stressed.

- **West (Air)** – The West is also associated with mental health and emotional balance. It governs relationships and communication, both of which are crucial for overall well-being. Keeping this zone in good shape is important for reducing stress and ensuring a calm environment for family members.

2. VASTU REMEDIES FOR BETTER HEALTH

While the principles of Vastu guide us toward creating a healthy environment, certain remedies can further enhance the energy flow and promote health.

COMMON VASTU REMEDIES FOR HEALTH:

- **Use of Plants**: Incorporating indoor plants in the north-east and east helps purify the air, increase oxygen levels, and promote a positive atmosphere. Plants like bamboo, money plants, and lavender can help balance the energy in your home or office.

- **Proper Ventilation**: Ensure that your space is well-ventilated and receives natural sunlight. This is crucial for ensuring proper air circulation and keeping the energy fresh and vibrant. Proper air flow can prevent the buildup of negative energy and promote mental and physical clarity.

- **Water Elements**: The North-East is the ideal direction to place water-related elements like fountains, aquariums, or even water bowls with fresh flowers. Water represents calmness, refreshment, and growth, and placing it in the right zone can help heal and rejuvenate the environment.

- **Declutter and Organize**: Clutter can cause stagnation in the energy flow, which directly affects health. It is important to maintain a clean and organized environment, especially in the north-east and south-east zones, to facilitate energy movement and create a serene atmosphere.

- **Colors for Health**: Colors have a significant impact on the energy of a space, and choosing the right colors for your home or workspace can boost your health. Soft blues and greens can be used in the north-east to promote healing and tranquility. Soft whites and yellows in the east can enhance energy and vitality.

- **Sleeping Direction**: For better health, Vastu suggests that one should sleep with their head facing the south or east. This helps align the body with the magnetic fields of the earth and promotes better sleep quality and overall well-being.

- **Air Purifiers**: In areas where natural airflow is limited, it's advisable to use air purifiers, especially in sleeping and workspaces. Ensuring the air is clean and fresh enhances overall health.

3. THE ROLE OF ASTROLOGY AND VASTU IN HEALTH

Incorporating Astro Vedic insights into Vastu practices helps customize solutions for health based on an individual's astrological chart. By considering the position of planets and astrological signs, you can determine which directions are most beneficial for your personal health.

- **Moon**: The Moon governs the mind, and its positioning in your astrological chart can influence emotional health. For mental well-being, the north-east direction is highly recommended for sleeping and relaxation.

- **Mars**: Mars is associated with strength and vitality, making the south-east an important direction for boosting physical health and digestion.

- **Saturn**: Saturn is linked with discipline, endurance, and long-term health. Its influence can be strengthened by spending time in the north-west direction, which promotes mental clarity and focus.

CASE STUDY: HEALING THROUGH VASTU

Client: Mr. S, 50, an entrepreneur facing frequent health issues, including stress, fatigue, and digestive disorders.

Issue: Mr. S reported constant fatigue and frequent stomach-related problems. He had trouble concentrating at work and was feeling emotionally drained.

ANALYSIS:

Mr. S's office was located in the south-west, which disrupted his energy flow, leading to emotional and physical instability. The south-east area was cluttered, and he had no exposure to sunlight in the office.

His bedroom had a cluttered north-east corner, and the head of his bed was facing the north, leading to disturbed sleep patterns.

SOLUTION:

We advised shifting his office desk to the north-east, allowing him better alignment with the water element for mental clarity.

He was encouraged to place a small aquarium in the north-east corner and a green plant in the east to enhance vitality.

We recommended placing his bed with the head facing south for improved sleep and recovery.

OUTCOME:

Within a few weeks, Mr. S experienced a noticeable improvement in his energy levels and digestive health. He reported a better sense of mental clarity and fewer bouts of stress.

CONCLUSION

Health is an intrinsic part of life, and Vastu Shastra offers an invaluable guide to creating a healing environment that supports your well-being. By understanding the role of different directions, applying Vastu remedies, and considering the influences of Astro Vedic principles, you can create spaces that not only improve your physical health but also contribute to your mental and emotional well-being.

The correct application of Vastu can lead to better **sleep**, **reduced stress**, and overall **mental clarity**, creating an environment that nurtures both body and mind for a healthier, more fulfilling life.

CHAPTER 11: THE ROLE OF VASTU IN RELATIONSHIPS AND FAMILY HARMONY

INTRODUCTION

One of the lesser-known but highly impactful areas of Vastu Shastra is its influence on **relationships** and **family dynamics**. The spaces where we live play a pivotal role in shaping how we interact with those around us. A harmonious home, aligned with Vastu principles, can foster **love**, **understanding**, and **communication** between family members. In contrast, poor Vastu can lead to conflict, misunderstanding, and strained relationships.

This chapter explores how the application of Vastu can enhance the **quality of relationships**, promote **harmony**, and ensure emotional well-being among family members. We'll also delve into how **Astro Vedic** principles can be incorporated to personalize solutions based on individual family members' astrological charts.

THE INFLUENCE OF VASTU ON FAMILY DYNAMICS

1. UNDERSTANDING THE ROLE OF DIFFERENT DIRECTIONS IN FAMILY HARMONY

Each direction in Vastu is connected to a particular aspect of family life, from the **overall health** of the family to the **relationship dynamics** between members. Proper alignment and attention to these directions can create a space that supports communication, cooperation, and **mutual respect** among family members.

KEY DIRECTIONS FOR FAMILY RELATIONSHIPS:

- **North-East (Spirituality & Mental Peace)**: The **north-east** is considered the most auspicious direction for nurturing **mental peace** and **spiritual growth**. A clean and positive north-east area in your home enhances **emotional stability**, making it an ideal space for prayer, meditation, and reflection. In the family context, this space can promote an atmosphere of understanding and emotional well-being, essential for healthy relationships.

- **East (Energy & Vitality)**: The **east** direction is the source of **sunlight** and **fresh air**, making it the perfect zone to keep the **living room** or **family room**. A family that spends time together in a well-lit and ventilated space will naturally experience better communication and emotional bonding. It enhances **optimism** and **positivity**, which are essential for harmony within the family.

- **South-West (Stability & Strength)**: This direction governs the **stability** of the family unit. A strong **south-west corner** provides a sense of security, which is essential for emotional well-being. In families, it is vital that parents, especially the **mother** and **father**, have a solid foundation in their relationship. The **south-west** strengthens relationships by providing a balanced and supportive environment.

- **South (Energy of Authority)**: The **south** direction is associated with **authority, leadership**, and **discipline**. In families, this zone helps reinforce the family's foundation of respect for authority. It is crucial to maintain balance in the **south** to avoid conflicts related to authority, especially between parents and children. A well-maintained south side enhances mutual respect and understanding in the family.

- **West (Communication & Relationships)**: The **west** direction influences family relationships and communication. If this area is kept positive and free of clutter, it can greatly enhance **clarity** and **open communication** among family members. Proper alignment and energy flow in the west can foster healthier dialogue and understanding between couples and between parents and children.

2. VASTU REMEDIES FOR STRENGTHENING FAMILY BONDS

In addition to the directions, Vastu provides several **remedies** that can be employed to create an atmosphere of love, understanding, and peace in the family.

COMMON VASTU REMEDIES FOR FAMILY HARMONY:

- **Use of Family Photos**: Displaying **family photos** in the **north-west** and **south-west** zones can create a strong sense of togetherness and emotional attachment. It helps remind family members of their deep connections and shared bonds.

- **Place of Worship**: A dedicated space for **prayer** and **meditation** in the **north-east** direction will encourage spiritual growth and a sense of togetherness. It allows each family member to reflect and develop individually, while simultaneously fostering collective harmony.

- **Furniture Arrangement**: The positioning of furniture can greatly influence family dynamics. Ensure that furniture is not blocking pathways in common areas, as blocked energy flow can create tensions and misunderstandings. **Circular seating** arrangements in the **living room** or **dining area** promote openness and equality, ensuring that each family member feels valued and heard.

- **Balanced Bedroom Layout**: For couples, placing the **bed** in the **south-west** with the **head towards the south** ensures stability and strengthens the relationship. Avoid placing the bed directly under an overhead beam, as this can create emotional strain or conflict.

- **Keep Clutter to a Minimum**: **Clutter** in the **living spaces** or **bedrooms** can lead to emotional chaos. Regular cleaning and organizing help maintain a positive environment. A clutter-free home promotes mental clarity, reduces stress, and creates a calm space where everyone can focus on building their relationships.

3. ASTRO VEDIC INFLUENCE ON RELATIONSHIPS

In addition to the physical environment, **Astro Vedic** insights can be applied to further personalize the solutions based on each family member's astrological chart. By understanding the specific energies and planetary influences of each individual, you can identify the ideal **directions** and **spaces** in the home that support their emotional and relationship growth.

- **Venus**: The planet Venus governs **love** and **relationships**. If Venus is prominent in an individual's chart, it suggests the need for a loving and harmonious environment. In such cases, the **south-west** and **north-west** zones should be enhanced with soft colors, flowers, and elements that promote **emotional stability**.

- **Mars**: Mars, the planet of **action** and **energy**, is important in family relationships where **discipline** and **leadership** play a role. If Mars is strong in the family member's astrological chart, the **south-east** should be carefully activated with vibrant energy, as it represents strength and vitality.

- **Moon**: The Moon influences **mental peace** and emotional balance. If a family member has a strong Moon influence, placing them in the **north-east** or **east** direction can enhance their emotional well-being. The Moon's calming effect will help maintain a peaceful atmosphere and reduce emotional turbulence.

- **Mercury**: Mercury governs **communication**. If Mercury is strong in a family member's chart, enhancing the **west** with **clear communication spaces** can lead to improved dialogue and better understanding between family members. It also helps in resolving conflicts and promoting open conversations.

4. CASE STUDY: HARMONIZING FAMILY DYNAMICS THROUGH VASTU

Client: The Soni family, consisting of parents and two children, were facing regular conflicts due to miscommunication, stress, and frequent misunderstandings. The father had a strong presence in the family, but this often led to tension between him and his children. The mother was experiencing emotional instability, and the children had difficulty expressing their thoughts.

ANALYSIS:

- The **living room** was in the **south-east**, leading to increased tension and frustration.

- The **family room** was cluttered with too many items in the **north-west**, making communication difficult.

- The **parents' bedroom** was in the **north-east**, which led to emotional instability for the mother.

SOLUTION:

- We moved the **living room** to the **east**, ensuring that it was filled with sunlight and air. This helped improve energy flow and contributed to more positive interactions.

- We cleared the **north-west** and placed family photographs to strengthen their bond.

- We recommended shifting the **parents' bedroom** to the **south-west** with the bed facing south for stability and harmony.

OUTCOME:

After making the changes, the family noticed a significant improvement in communication and emotional stability. The mother felt more grounded, and the father experienced less conflict with the children. The children were more expressive, and overall family dynamics became more peaceful.

CONCLUSION

Vastu Shastra offers more than just design and aesthetics; it provides a framework for creating **harmonious relationships** and fostering **family unity**. By aligning the spaces in the home according to Vastu principles, we can create an environment that supports open communication, emotional stability, and mutual respect. When combined with **Astro Vedic** insights, it provides a personalized approach to nurturing and strengthening familial bonds. A harmonious home can lead to a harmonious life—one filled with love, respect, and understanding.

CHAPTER 12: VASTU FOR PROSPERITY AND ABUNDANCE

INTRODUCTION

Prosperity and **abundance** are goals that many strive for, but achieving them requires more than just effort and hard work. In Vastu Shastra, the spaces where we live, work, and engage in our daily activities hold immense power in determining the flow of **positive energy** (also known as **prana**) that leads to financial and personal success. This chapter focuses on how Vastu principles can be utilized to attract **prosperity**, improve **financial stability**, and foster **overall abundance** in life.

When combined with **Astro Vedic** techniques, these principles can be further personalized to create a comprehensive strategy that enhances an individual's potential for success.

THE VASTU FRAMEWORK FOR PROSPERITY

In Vastu Shastra, the balance of the **five elements** (earth, water, fire, air, and ether) within the home or workspace plays a crucial role in influencing the energy flow that supports prosperity. Certain directions and areas of your environment are believed to impact **wealth** and **success,** and understanding how to optimize these spaces can enhance your ability to attract financial abundance.

1. KEY DIRECTIONS AND THEIR ROLE IN PROSPERITY

- **North (Wealth and Career)**: The **north** direction is most strongly associated with **prosperity** and **career growth**. According to Vastu, the **north-east** is the most powerful zone for financial success, as it is linked to the **planet Mercury**, which governs wealth and trade. A clean and positive environment in the **north-east** will boost one's ability to attract wealth and opportunities.

- **North-East (Success and Financial Growth)**: As mentioned earlier, the **north-east** is the best direction for success and prosperity. This area represents **God's blessings, knowledge**, and **spiritual progress**, which can help individuals align themselves with the energies that attract abundance. The presence of **a clear space** or **a prayer area** in the north-east corner helps to foster positive financial energy.

- **South-East (Wealth and Prosperity)**: The **south-east** governs the **fire element**, which is linked to energy, action, and wealth accumulation. Keeping the **south-east** area clean, bright, and energized is important for **prosperity**. The **south-east** is considered the **money zone**, and enhancing this space with colors like **red, orange**, and **green** can promote wealth.

- **West (Reputation and Networking)**: The **west** direction influences **reputation, growth**, and **networking**. For business owners or individuals looking to enhance their professional reputation and establish connections, focusing on this area can be beneficial. Proper lighting and cleanliness in the west encourage smooth business relationships, which are vital for prosperity.

VASTU REMEDIES FOR ATTRACTING PROSPERITY

In addition to understanding the significance of key directions, there are several **Vastu remedies** that can be used to amplify the positive energies in your environment and invite prosperity and abundance.

1. ENTRANCE AND MAIN DOOR

The **main entrance** to your home or office is one of the most important aspects of **Vastu**. This is the **gateway for all energies** entering your space, and it should be designed in a way that welcomes **positive energy**.

- The **main door** should be located in the **north, north-east,** or **east** directions. These directions invite wealth and prosperity, making it easier for positive energies to enter and for financial growth to follow.

- Ensure that the **main door** is free of obstacles, **clean,** and **well-lit**. Avoid placing any **heavy objects** or **clutter** around the entrance. An unimpeded, welcoming door sets the stage for abundance to enter your life.

2. USE OF WATER FEATURES

Water is a powerful element associated with **flow** and **prosperity**. In Vastu, **water** symbolizes **fluidity** and **wealth,** and it plays an important role in attracting prosperity.

- A **small water fountain** or **aquarium** in the **north** or **north-east** can significantly increase the flow of prosperity. The sound and presence of water enhance the flow of positive energy, which can help in manifesting financial success.

- However, it is important to keep the water clean and free of stagnation. A stagnant water feature may symbolize a **blockage** in the flow of wealth, so regular maintenance is essential.

3. COLORS AND DECORATIONS FOR PROSPERITY

Vastu recommends certain **colors** and **decorative elements** to enhance the flow of prosperity.

- **Green** is often associated with **growth, abundance**, and **success**. It is recommended to use **green** plants or **green-colored décor** in the **south-east** or **north-east** directions to promote wealth.

- **Gold** and **yellow** are considered colors of **prosperity** and **luxury**. If you are looking to enhance **financial abundance**, it is wise to incorporate these colors in your **living room** or **office** space.

- **Crystals** like **amethyst** or **jade** are known to attract **prosperity**. Placing them in the **south-east** or **north-east** can significantly increase positive energy and help in manifesting wealth.

4. PLACEMENT OF WEALTH SYMBOLS

In Vastu Shastra, certain symbols are believed to bring prosperity and wealth when placed in specific areas of the house. These include:

- **A statue of Lord Ganesha**: Ganesha is widely regarded as the **remover of obstacles** and the **god of wealth**. Placing a statue of Ganesha at the **north-east** direction is considered highly auspicious for attracting prosperity.

- **A money plant**: The **money plant** is said to invite wealth and financial success when placed in the **south-east** zone.

It is a symbol of growing wealth and abundant opportunities.

- **A mirror**: A mirror in the **North** can reflect wealth and success. Ensure that the mirror is placed in such a way that it does not reflect any **clutter** or **garbage**, as it may reflect negative energies back into the space.

ASTRO VEDIC APPROACHES FOR WEALTH AND PROSPERITY

Incorporating **Astro Vedic** techniques into Vastu remedies for prosperity can provide more tailored solutions based on the unique **astrological chart** of the individual. By understanding the influence of **planets** and **dasha periods**, you can strengthen the flow of wealth according to the personal astrological influences.

KEY ASTRO VEDIC INSIGHTS FOR PROSPERITY:

- **Mercury**: Mercury governs **business** and **communication**, making it an essential planet for **financial success**. If Mercury is strong in an individual's chart, it can enhance skills related to business management, trade, and communication. Strengthening the **north-east** direction and incorporating **greenery** can increase Mercury's positive influence.

- **Jupiter**: Jupiter is the planet of **growth**, **expansion**, and **abundance**. If Jupiter is well-placed in the individual's chart, they will naturally experience financial growth. In such cases, enhancing the **north-east** area and ensuring it is filled with **natural light** can encourage prosperity.

- **Saturn**: Saturn governs **hard work** and **discipline**. If Saturn is influencing your chart in a positive way, maintaining a **clean and organized workspace** can help you achieve long-term prosperity. The **south-west** direction is best suited for people influenced by Saturn, as it helps provide the **stability** required for achieving wealth.

CASE STUDY: ATTRACTING PROSPERITY WITH VASTU

Client: The Khurana family had been running a business for over a decade but were struggling to achieve the financial success they desired. They noticed that despite working hard, the flow of money into their business was erratic and inconsistent.

ANALYSIS:

- The **main entrance** to their office was in the **south-west** zone, which obstructed the flow of positive financial energy.

- The **south-east** area was cluttered, and there were no water features or elements to enhance the **fire element** associated with wealth.

SOLUTION:

- We shifted the main entrance to the **north-east** and made it more welcoming by cleaning and organizing the space.

- The **south-east** was cleared, and a **water fountain** was added to increase prosperity.

- The family placed a **statue of Lord Ganesha** in the **north-east** area and added **green plants** in the **south-east**.

OUTCOME:

Within a few months, the Khuranas noticed a significant increase in business transactions and steady financial growth. Their office environment became more dynamic and positive, with an enhanced flow of opportunities.

CONCLUSION

Incorporating **Vastu** principles into your home or workspace is an incredibly effective way to create an environment that attracts **prosperity** and **financial success**. By enhancing the key areas associated with wealth, clearing blockages, and incorporating **Astro Vedic** insights into the design of your space, you can pave the way for a life filled with abundance. When the environment is aligned with natural energies, prosperity flows effortlessly.

CHAPTER 13: VASTU AND HEALTH – THE VITAL CONNECTION

INTRODUCTION

In the pursuit of **prosperity** and **success**, health often becomes the foundation upon which everything else stands. **Good health** is not just the absence of illness but a **balance** between the mind, body, and spirit. Vastu Shastra provides significant insights into how our living and working spaces influence our **physical** and **mental well-being**. When designed and aligned properly, our environment can enhance energy flow, reduce stress, and improve overall health.

In this chapter, we will explore how the principles of Vastu can be used to promote **better health**, enhance **vitality**, and ensure **long-term wellness**. Additionally, we will discuss how **Astro Vedic** techniques can be integrated into the Vastu framework to further personalize health solutions based on individual astrological charts.

THE VASTU FRAMEWORK FOR HEALTH

The **five elements – earth, water, fire, air**, and **ether** – each play an important role in creating a balanced environment. The alignment of these elements in your living and working spaces can have profound effects on your **physical, mental**, and **emotional health**. A well-balanced space helps to **reduce stress**, promotes **relaxation**, and boosts overall **well-being**.

1. KEY DIRECTIONS AND THEIR IMPACT ON HEALTH

- **North-East (Mind and Body Balance)**: The **north-east** direction is associated with the **water element** and represents a space for **mental clarity** and **emotional well-being**. Ensuring this direction is clear, open, and filled with natural light can help create a peaceful environment conducive to good health.

- **South-West (Stability and Rest)**: The **south-west** direction is considered the **earth element**, which brings **stability** and **groundedness**. This area is especially important for ensuring restful sleep, relaxation, and overall health. A bedroom in the **south-west** helps in maintaining mental peace and provides the foundation for good health.

- **East (Energy and Vitality)**: The **east** is a direction of **renewal** and **vitality**, governed by the **air element**. Sunlight, fresh air, and natural elements in the **east** can help boost energy levels, improve immunity, and maintain overall health. A **well-ventilated** and **bright** space in the **east** is ideal for boosting the body's energy.

VASTU REMEDIES FOR HEALTH AND WELLNESS

While each direction has a distinct influence on health, there are also specific **Vastu remedies** to enhance your living environment and improve overall well-being.

1. PROPER VENTILATION AND LIGHT

Natural light and fresh air are two of the most important factors for a healthy living space. In **Vastu Shastra**, the **east** direction is the best for **sunlight**. Ensure that your home or office space receives ample **daylight**, especially in areas where you spend most of your time.

- **Windows and Ventilation**: Keep the windows in the **east** and **north** open during the day to allow natural light and air to flow freely through the space. **Good ventilation** helps in maintaining a clean environment by flushing out stale air and preventing the build-up of harmful gases.

- **Aromatic Plants**: Incorporating plants like **basil, tulsi**, and **aloe vera** can not only improve the quality of air but also help purify the environment, promoting good health. These plants can be placed in the **north-east** or **east** direction to enhance the **life force energy**.

2. DECLUTTER FOR MENTAL PEACE

Clutter is a silent yet powerful disruptor of good health. In **Vastu, clutter** creates negative energy and can lead to **mental stress** and **physical ailments**.

- **De-clutter your home or office** by organizing spaces and removing items that are no longer needed. This will not only create a more organized and peaceful environment but will also ensure that the **flow of positive energy** is unhindered.

- **Keep the bedroom free of clutter**. The **south-west** corner of the bedroom, especially, should be a **quiet and serene space**, free of distractions, to ensure that the mind can relax and rejuvenate during sleep.

3. BEDROOM VASTU FOR RESTFUL SLEEP

The **bedroom** is a crucial area when it comes to health. Poor sleep quality can directly impact mental clarity, energy levels, and overall well-being. Ensuring that the bedroom is aligned according to **Vastu principles** is vital for good health.

- **South-West for the Master Bedroom**: The **south-west** direction is ideal for the **master bedroom**, as it promotes stability and restful sleep. Avoid placing the bed directly under a window or ceiling fan. This helps in maintaining a restful environment and prevents disruptions during sleep.

- **Position of the Bed**: Place the bed in such a way that when you lie down, your **head faces the south or east**, and your feet face the **north** or **west**. This alignment ensures proper circulation of energy during rest.

- **Avoid electronics near the bed**: Keep electronic gadgets like **televisions, mobile phones**, and **computers** away from the bedroom to prevent interference with the body's natural energy and reduce exposure to electromagnetic radiation.

4. USE OF WATER FEATURES FOR HEALING

Water is a healing element, and its presence can contribute to physical and emotional well-being. In Vastu, water symbolizes both **flow** and **purity**, two essential elements for good health.

- **Water Fountains**: A small **water fountain** in the **north-east** or **north** direction can help improve the flow of positive energy and enhance mental clarity. The sound of water has a **calming effect** on the mind, helping to reduce stress and promote relaxation.

- **Aquariums**: **Aquariums** are a popular way to bring the healing energy of water into your home. The placement of an aquarium in the **north-east** direction is beneficial for bringing prosperity and mental peace.

- **Avoid Stagnant Water**: In Vastu, stagnant water is considered a **negative** element that can lead to physical discomfort, illness, and poor energy flow. Ensure that there are no **stagnant water pools** around the home or workspace.

5. ASTRO VEDIC APPROACHES TO HEALTH

When integrating **Astro Vedic** techniques into Vastu remedies, individuals can receive personalized insights into how their **astrological chart** impacts their health and well-being. Each **planetary influence** and **dasha period** affects health in different ways, and understanding these influences can guide Vastu solutions that are more specific and targeted.

KEY ASTRO VEDIC INSIGHTS FOR HEALTH:

- **Sun**: The **Sun** represents vitality, energy, and overall health. If the **Sun** is strong in an individual's chart, they will experience good physical health and energy levels. Enhancing the **east** direction with **bright light** and ensuring a good flow of energy will support the positive influence of the **Sun**.

- **Moon**: The **Moon** governs the **mind, emotions,** and **mental health**. If the **Moon** is prominent in your chart, focus on creating a **calm, serene environment** in the **north-east** or **east** for emotional balance and mental well-being. A **water fountain** in this area can help soothe the mind.

- **Mars**: Mars represents **energy, strength**, and **vitality**. If Mars is influencing your chart, it is important to maintain an active lifestyle and promote **physical fitness**. Placing plants and having an active space in the **south-east** area can enhance the influence of Mars.

CASE STUDY: IMPROVING HEALTH WITH VASTU

Client: Mrs. Sharma, a 42-year-old executive, had been experiencing **chronic stress** and poor sleep patterns, which were negatively impacting her overall health. She approached us to assess her home and work environment for Vastu corrections.

ANALYSIS:

The **bedroom** was located in the **north-west** direction, which disrupted the restful energy needed for deep sleep.

The **east** direction of her home was cluttered, blocking the flow of positive energy, leading to a lack of mental clarity.

SOLUTION:

We recommended shifting her **bedroom** to the **south-west** and ensuring her bed faced the **south** to improve sleep quality.

The **east** was cleared of clutter, and **green plants** were added to promote fresh energy.

A **small water fountain** was placed in the **north-east** for mental peace and clarity.

OUTCOME:

Within weeks, Mrs. Sharma experienced improved sleep, reduced stress, and a significant boost in her overall energy levels. Her productivity at work also improved, and she felt more focused and at peace.

CONCLUSION

Incorporating **Vastu** principles into the design of your home or office can significantly enhance your **health** and **well-being**. By aligning the five elements, optimizing key directions, and incorporating **Astro Vedic** remedies, individuals can foster a healthy environment that supports both physical vitality and mental peace. When the spaces around us are harmonious, our own health flourishes, making it easier to pursue success and happiness in every aspect of life.

CHAPTER 14: VASTU FOR PROSPERITY AND WEALTH

INTRODUCTION

Wealth is not just about **money** or **material possessions**, but also about the **abundance** of opportunities, positive energy, and **success** in all areas of life. In **Vastu Shastra**, prosperity is believed to be deeply influenced by the flow of energy within our environment. Proper alignment of space, the placement of key elements, and mindful positioning can significantly impact our ability to attract wealth, success, and opportunities.

This chapter explores the principles of **Vastu** for wealth, prosperity, and **financial success**. Additionally, it delves into how **Astro Vedic** techniques can be applied to further personalize the environment based on the individual's **astrological chart**, enhancing their path toward abundance.

THE VASTU FRAMEWORK FOR PROSPERITY

According to **Vastu Shastra**, the flow of energy in your living and working spaces must be optimized to invite **positive vibrations** that can bring prosperity and wealth. The arrangement of the **five elements** (earth, water, fire, air, and ether) plays a crucial role in shaping the **energy balance** required for attracting wealth.

1. THE ROLE OF DIRECTIONS IN WEALTH ATTRACTION

- **North (The Direction of Wealth)**: The **north** is the most auspicious direction for attracting **wealth** and **prosperity**, as it is associated with the **Kubera**, the Hindu god of wealth. The **north** is ruled by **water**, which represents abundance, flow, and continuous growth. Keeping this direction **clear** and **clutter-free** helps in the continuous flow of wealth into your life.

- **North-East (Spiritual Prosperity)**: The **north-east** direction symbolizes **spiritual growth** and **wisdom**. While it is more commonly associated with mental peace and clarity, its role in **prosperity** cannot be overlooked. A well-balanced **north-east** ensures the right **mental attitude** towards attracting wealth and the ability to seize new opportunities when they arise.

- **South-East (The Direction of Fire and Activity)**: The **south-east** direction represents the **fire element**, which is vital for **action** and **growth**. It is directly related to **financial transactions** and **business activities**. Placing important financial documents, business dealings, or wealth-related symbols like a **safe** in the **south-east** can boost prosperity in business and financial matters.

- **South-West (Stability and Grounding)**: The **south-west** direction governs **stability** and **grounding**, both of which are necessary for maintaining the wealth once it has been acquired. It is essential that the **south-west corner** of your home or office remains stable and free from clutter, ensuring that the wealth you attract stays grounded and protected.

VASTU REMEDIES FOR WEALTH AND PROSPERITY

Incorporating specific **Vastu remedies** in your home or workspace can facilitate the flow of positive energy and prosperity. These solutions can be simple yet powerful, having a significant impact on your financial success.

1. MAIN ENTRANCE AND WEALTH FLOW

- The **main entrance** is the **gateway** for all energy to enter your space, including **financial prosperity**. A clean, well-lit, and welcoming entrance ensures that the right kind of energy flows into your space.

- **North Entrance**: Ideally, the **main door** should be located in the **north** or **north-east** direction, as this maximizes the flow of wealth energy into your space. Avoid placing the main entrance in the **south-west** as it may block the prosperity flow.

- **Symbolic Elements**: Placing symbols of **prosperity** like a **money plant**, **Lord Ganesha** idol, or **elephant figurines** at the entrance can invite wealth and abundance. Ensure these symbols face inward, welcoming wealth into your life.

- **Avoid Clutter at the Entrance**: Cluttered entrances block the flow of wealth energy. Keep the area around your **main door** tidy and free from obstructions.

2. PLACEMENT OF WEALTH-RELATED SYMBOLS

- Specific symbols of wealth and abundance can amplify the energy of prosperity. These symbols can be placed in strategic locations based on **Vastu** principles to invite wealth and opportunities.

- **Safe or Cash Box**: The **south-east** corner is ideal for placing a **safe, cash box**, or **bank documents**. This placement ensures that your financial assets are protected and stored in an environment that supports growth.

- **Money Plant**: The **money plant** is considered an auspicious symbol of wealth in **Vastu**. It should be placed in the **north-east** or **north** direction to ensure prosperity and financial stability. Be sure to take good care of the plant, as its health is believed to reflect the flow of wealth.

- **Mirror**: A **mirror** in the **north** direction reflects and amplifies wealth. It should be clean, well-maintained, and placed in a way that it reflects positive energy into the space.

3. ENSURE PROPER VENTILATION AND LIGHT

Natural light and **ventilation** are essential in ensuring that the energy flow is balanced and invigorating. The **south-east** area, which corresponds to **fire**, should be well-lit with natural sunlight or bright artificial lighting. This energizes the space and ensures **constant action** and **growth**.

- **Windows**: Ensure windows are kept open during the day to let in sunlight and fresh air. The **north** and **east** directions should have larger windows for this purpose.

- **Lighting**: Bright lights in the **south-east** or **north** direction can help in maximizing wealth and prosperity.

4. CLUTTER-FREE SPACES FOR CLEAR INTENTIONS

Clutter is a major obstacle in the flow of positive energy and can lead to stagnation in financial affairs. Keep spaces free from unnecessary items and ensure that everything has a place. This allows wealth to flow freely and unhindered.

- **Declutter the South-West**: This area, representing stability, should be clear of unnecessary items to ensure that the wealth and prosperity you attract are stable and long-lasting.

- **Organize the Office or Work Desk**: Keep your **work desk** or **office space** organized. This is especially important for individuals in business or financial professions, as it helps in channeling focus and intention towards generating wealth.

ASTRO VEDIC INSIGHTS FOR FINANCIAL PROSPERITY

While **Vastu** is an important tool for attracting wealth, it can be even more effective when combined with **Astro Vedic** insights. Your **birth chart** provides valuable information about your financial potential, career prospects, and overall wealth.

KEY ASTRO VEDIC FACTORS:

- **Sun's Position**: The **Sun** is the primary source of energy and vitality. Its position in your chart indicates your **confidence**, **leadership**, and ability to attract success. A strong Sun placement can bring abundant wealth and the ability to shine in your professional life.

- **Venus (Shukra)**: Venus governs **luxury**, **material wealth**, and **beauty**. A favorable placement of Venus in your chart can indicate an affinity for wealth, art, and fine living. Strengthening the **north-east** or **north** area in your space can further enhance Venus' favorable influence.

- **Jupiter (Guru)**: Jupiter is the planet of **abundance** and **growth**. A well-placed Jupiter can ensure **financial gains** and **prosperity**. You can strengthen Jupiter's influence by placing **symbols of wealth** and **good fortune** in the **north-east** or **east** directions.

CASE STUDY: ATTRACTING WEALTH THROUGH VASTU

Client: Mr. Ramesh, a 38-year-old businessman, had been facing stagnation in his business for several years. Despite having a good reputation, he was struggling with **financial losses** and missed opportunities.

ANALYSIS:

The **north** direction of his office was cluttered and blocked by heavy furniture, preventing the smooth flow of **wealth energy**.

The **south-east** corner, which governs **action** and **business**, was occupied by an outdated printer and an unused storage cabinet.

SOLUTION:

The **north** was cleared, ensuring a free flow of positive energy.

The **south-east** area was cleared and redesigned to hold a **safe** and **cash register**.

We also placed a **money plant** in the **north-east** of his office to enhance prosperity.

OUTCOME:

Within two months, Mr. Ramesh saw a significant **increase in business**. New opportunities came his way, and he made a major contract deal that turned his financial situation around. The changes brought prosperity and renewed success to his business.

CONCLUSION

Wealth is not just a product of hard work and determination, but also of the environment you create around you. **Vastu Shastra** provides us with the tools to create spaces that invite wealth, prosperity, and success into our lives. By optimizing key directions, utilizing the right symbols, and integrating **Astro Vedic** principles, we can align ourselves with the energies of abundance and ensure that we attract prosperity with ease.

As you apply these principles to your own home or workspace, you will find that the flow of wealth becomes effortless, and financial opportunities present themselves in abundance.

CHAPTER 15: THE IMPACT OF VASTU ON RELATIONSHIPS

INTRODUCTION

The energy within your home or workspace not only affects your financial success but also plays a significant role in shaping the relationships you experience. **Vastu Shastra** is based on the principle that our environment directly influences our physical, emotional, and mental well-being. Similarly, it impacts the harmony, communication, and balance within our personal relationships, be it family, friends, or romantic partners.

In this chapter, we will explore how the application of **Vastu** principles can positively influence your relationships, create a peaceful atmosphere in your home, and foster mutual respect, love, and understanding. We will also incorporate insights from **Astro Vedic** techniques to tailor these remedies based on individual astrological placements.

THE ROLE OF VASTU IN RELATIONSHIP HARMONY

1. THE IMPORTANCE OF THE BEDROOM

The **bedroom** is a private space that symbolizes emotional intimacy, rest, and rejuvenation. In **Vastu**, the arrangement and energy in the bedroom play a crucial role in fostering harmony, respect, and affection in relationships.

- **Positioning of the Bed**: According to **Vastu**, the **bed** should ideally be placed in the **south-west** corner of the room. This corner represents **stability** and **grounding**, which helps in fostering long-lasting relationships. The bed should be placed in a way that both partners can sleep with their heads towards the **south** or **east** for a restful and rejuvenating sleep.

- **Avoiding Overhead Beams**: Overhead beams in the **bedroom** can create an oppressive atmosphere, leading to unnecessary tension in relationships. If you cannot avoid overhead beams, use **curtains** or **drapes** to shield them.

- **Colors and Décor**: Choose **soothing** and **warm** colors for the bedroom to create a calm, peaceful, and loving atmosphere. Light shades of **blue**, **lavender**, **peach**, and **green** are ideal as they promote relaxation and positive energy.

2. THE LIVING ROOM AND SOCIAL INTERACTIONS

The **living room** is the space where we spend time with family and guests. It is essential that this area supports healthy communication, understanding, and connection among family members and friends.

- **Arrangement of Seating**: In the **living room**, seating should be arranged to promote **open communication** and equality. The seating should be placed in such a way that all members of the family can face each other comfortably. This encourages conversation and mutual respect. Avoid placing chairs with their backs to the door, as it can create discomfort and insecurity.

- **Symbols of Unity**: Adding symbols such as a **family photo**, a **love symbol**, or even a **peaceful landscape painting** can help promote positive energy. Such symbols act as reminders of unity, love, and connection.

- **Avoid Clutter**: Just as clutter in the home can obstruct the flow of wealth, it also blocks the flow of positive energy necessary for harmonious relationships. Keeping the living room clutter-free ensures that energy flows freely, allowing for peaceful interactions.

VASTU FOR STRENGTHENING MARITAL RELATIONSHIPS

A strong marital relationship requires emotional, mental, and spiritual alignment. Vastu can support this alignment by ensuring that the physical environment nurtures love, trust, and respect.

1. AVOIDING NEGATIVE ENERGY

Negative energy can manifest in various forms, such as **arguments**, **misunderstandings**, or **lack of communication**. The primary cause for this in the home is often an imbalance in the energy of the space.

- **Mirrors in the Bedroom**: Mirrors in the bedroom should be used carefully. A mirror directly facing the bed may lead to emotional disturbances or confusion. It is advisable to place mirrors in areas where they reflect **positive energy** such as the **living room** or the **dining area**.

- **Unnecessary Separation**: Avoid placing two single beds in the bedroom unless absolutely necessary. Two separate beds can create a feeling of separation in a marital relationship. If space is an issue, try to make use of **foldable beds** or **sofa beds** that can be adjusted based on your needs.

2. CREATING POSITIVE ENERGY WITH NATURAL ELEMENTS

Introducing natural elements into your home can help create an environment that supports love and harmony. Here are a few **Vastu** tips for incorporating these elements:

- **Water Elements**: The element of water is known to represent flow, abundance, and emotional healing. Place a **water fountain** or a **small fish tank** in the **north-east** or **east** of your living room to encourage balance and harmony in relationships.

- **Wood and Plants**: Wood is symbolic of growth, stability, and fertility. Consider adding plants such as the **money plant** or **bamboo** in the **south-east** or **north-east** of your home to invite positive energy.

- **Crystals**: Crystals are believed to help clear negative energy and attract positive vibrations. **Rose quartz**, in particular, is a crystal known for its ability to attract love and harmony in relationships. Place **rose quartz** stones in the **bedroom** or **living room** to enhance the emotional energy of the space.

THE INFLUENCE OF DIRECTIONS ON RELATIONSHIP HEALTH

The direction in which specific rooms and items are placed is integral to maintaining harmony in relationships. Each direction governs different aspects of life and affects relationships in unique ways.

1. THE SOUTH-WEST DIRECTION

The **south-west** direction is the most important for stabilizing relationships. It governs the energy of **stability**, **trust**, and

longevity. For marital relationships, the **south-west** is the key direction to nurture.

- **Place the Bed in the South-West**: As mentioned before, the **south-west** corner should be reserved for the bed in a **master bedroom**, as it ensures the stability of the relationship. Avoid placing a bed in the **north-west** or **south-east** areas, as these can cause imbalance.

- **Family Unity**: The **south-west** is also the ideal place for family photographs or symbols that signify unity and connection. It helps strengthen the emotional bond between partners.

2. THE NORTH-EAST DIRECTION

The **north-east** is associated with mental clarity, spiritual growth, and wisdom. This direction can be highly beneficial for couples seeking deeper emotional and spiritual connection.

- **Meditation or Prayer Corner**: Consider placing a **meditation** or **prayer** space in the **north-east** of your home. This helps couples find peace and alignment in their relationship, fostering respect, patience, and understanding.

- **Avoid Overcrowding the North-East**: Overcrowding this area can lead to confusion and emotional unrest. Ensure that this area is kept open and clean to allow clarity and peaceful energy to flow.

ASTRO VEDIC INSIGHTS FOR RELATIONSHIP HARMONY

Incorporating **Astro Vedic** insights into Vastu can further personalize the remedies to suit individual needs. By aligning your home's energy with your **astrological chart**, you can strengthen relationships and ensure long-lasting peace.

KEY ASTRO VEDIC FACTORS:

Moon and Venus: The **Moon** represents emotions, while **Venus** governs love and relationships. The placement of the **Moon** and **Venus** in your birth chart can provide insight into the emotional needs of your relationships. These planets can also determine how you handle emotional challenges in relationships.

Mars and Saturn: These two planets play a significant role in **conflict resolution** and **strengthening emotional resilience**. The right placement of **Mars** can ensure that challenges are overcome with **strength** and **unity**, while Saturn encourages **commitment** and **patience**.

CASE STUDY: RESTORING HARMONY THROUGH VASTU

Client: Ms. Priya and Mr. Rajesh, a married couple, were facing constant arguments and misunderstandings. They were living in a newly renovated apartment, but their relationship had become strained over time. Despite their best efforts, they were unable to restore peace.

ANALYSIS:

- The couple's **bedroom** was located in the **north-west** corner, which created instability and emotional distance.

- The **south-west corner** of the bedroom was cluttered with old furniture and unnecessary items.

SOLUTION:

- We shifted their bed to the **south-west** corner to ensure stability.

- The clutter was removed, and they placed **family photographs** in the **south-west** of the bedroom.

- A **small water fountain** was added to the **north-east** of the living room to promote emotional healing.

OUTCOME:

Within a few weeks, Priya and Rajesh noticed a significant shift in their relationship. The energy in their home felt lighter, and their communication became more open and loving. The changes led to increased understanding and emotional connection, and their marital harmony was restored.

CONCLUSION

Vastu Shastra offers profound insights into improving relationships by creating an environment that fosters love, understanding, and emotional balance. When combined with **Astro Vedic** principles, Vastu remedies become even more personalized, aligning physical spaces with the individual's emotional and spiritual needs. By following these guidelines, you can create a space that enhances the quality of your relationships, ensuring peace, stability, and growth in your personal connections.

CHAPTER 16: THE ROLE OF VASTU IN CAREER AND SUCCESS

INTRODUCTION

Just as **Vastu Shastra** influences your home and relationships, it plays a pivotal role in your career and professional success. The environment you work in can significantly affect your productivity, creativity, and overall career growth. Vastu principles can help you set up your workspace in a way that attracts positive energy, clears obstacles, and fosters opportunities for advancement.

In this chapter, we will explore how **Vastu Shastra** can be applied to your professional life, from the arrangement of office spaces to optimizing energy flow, and how **Astro Vedic** insights can further enhance these practices for tailored solutions.

VASTU AND CAREER GROWTH

1. THE IMPORTANCE OF THE WORK DESK

Your desk or work area is a vital part of your professional life. This space should be aligned in a way that promotes focus, creativity, and success. According to **Vastu**, the arrangement of your desk influences how well you perform and the opportunities that come your way.

- **Positioning the Desk**: Ideally, your desk should face the **north** or **east** direction. These directions are associated with knowledge, prosperity, and career advancement. When sitting at your desk, you should have a solid **wall behind** you for support, symbolizing **security** and **stability** in your career.

- **Avoid Facing the Door**: In Vastu, sitting with your back to the door creates a sense of insecurity and vulnerability. It is better to have your desk positioned so that you can see the door without directly facing it, which allows you to stay alert to opportunities and challenges.

- **Clutter-Free Workspace**: A **cluttered desk** can lead to mental clutter, reducing focus and hindering productivity. Keep your workspace organized, with only essential items, to ensure a smooth flow of energy. Incorporate items that inspire success, like a **crystal**, a **plant**, or a **vision board**.

2. THE POWER OF THE OFFICE ENTRYWAY

The entryway to your office plays a key role in setting the tone for your workday and your professional journey. This is where **energy** enters, so it must be kept open and welcoming.

- **Clean and Inviting Entry**: The **north** or **east** side of the office should be clear of obstructions to ensure that positive energy flows freely. Avoid placing anything heavy or bulky near the entrance, as it can create an energy blockage.

- **Avoid Negative Symbols**: Be mindful of what you display in your office's entrance. Avoid **negative imagery** or anything that represents failure or confusion. Instead, opt for symbols of **success**, **growth**, and **prosperity**, such as a **mountain painting**, a **golden eagle**, or an **open road**.

VASTU FOR SPECIFIC CAREER PATHS

1. FOR ENTREPRENEURS AND BUSINESS OWNERS

Entrepreneurs need an environment that fosters creativity, decision-making, and business growth. Vastu can provide invaluable guidance for creating a workspace that supports these needs.

- **Business Setup**: The **south-west** corner of the office should be dedicated to the owner's desk to ensure power and stability. The business's **reception area** should be in the **north-east** or **north** direction to attract prosperity and new clients.

- **Finance and Accounts**: The **south-east** direction is associated with wealth and finances. Ensure that the finance or accounting section of your office is located here to help attract monetary success and financial clarity.

2. FOR CREATIVE PROFESSIONALS

For artists, writers, and creative professionals, it is crucial to have a space that encourages creativity and inspiration. According to Vastu, certain directions can influence your creative energies.

- **Creative Desk Location**: For a boost in creativity, place your desk in the **north-east** or **north-west** direction, which governs knowledge, intuition, and mental clarity.

- **Color and Décor**: The colors of your workspace can also impact your creative process. Shades of **blue**, **green**, and **yellow** help stimulate creative thinking. Keep your workspace neat, with **inspirational quotes** or **artworks** that motivate you.

3. FOR CAREER SEEKERS AND PROFESSIONALS

For those looking to advance in their careers or secure a new job, creating an environment that attracts opportunities and success is essential.

- **Job Search Desk**: Position your desk in the **north** or **east** direction to improve the chances of receiving job offers or career advancements. Keeping your desk organized, with a

crystal or a **vision board** that focuses on your career goals, can help attract positive energy.

- **Networking and Socializing**: Networking is a crucial part of career growth. The **south-east** direction is ideal for socializing, building relationships, and attracting professional connections. Set up a **meeting table** or **conference area** here to ensure a smooth flow of conversations.

THE IMPACT OF DIRECTIONS ON CAREER SUCCESS

The directional alignment of your workspace can significantly influence your career trajectory. In Vastu, different directions govern specific aspects of your professional life.

1. NORTH DIRECTION – THE SOURCE OF CAREER ADVANCEMENT

The **north** direction is ruled by **Mercury**, which governs wealth, prosperity, and career success. This direction is essential for business owners, professionals, and anyone seeking to climb the career ladder.

- **Desk Position**: The desk should ideally be placed in the **north** to attract prosperity and professional growth. The **north-east** is also favorable for increasing knowledge and opportunities.

- **Important Symbols**: For career success, display items that symbolize wealth and success, such as a **small water fountain** or a **crystal pyramid** in the **north** of your workspace.

2. SOUTH-WEST DIRECTION – THE SOURCE OF STABILITY AND POWER

The **south-west** direction is associated with stability, authority, and power. It is essential for anyone looking for long-term success in their careers or business.

- **Owner's Desk**: The desk of the **business owner** or **top executive** should be placed in the **south-west** corner of the office to ensure power and authority. This direction ensures that the business or individual is rooted in stability and long-term growth.

- **Leadership Display**: To reinforce this energy, you can display leadership symbols, such as **pictures of mentors, awards**, or **success certificates** in the **south-west**.

COMBINING VASTU WITH ASTRO VEDIC FOR CAREER SUCCESS

Aligning your workspace with your **astrological chart** can provide an added layer of customization to enhance career growth. The positions of your **Moon, Mercury**, and **Saturn** in your birth chart influence your work habits, communication, and long-term success.

KEY ASTRO VEDIC FACTORS:

- **Mercury's Influence**: Mercury governs **communication, intelligence**, and **business acumen**. If **Mercury** is strong in your chart, positioning your desk in the **north-east** or **north** will amplify your ability to communicate and succeed professionally.

- **Saturn's Influence**: Saturn is the planet of **discipline, hard work**, and **responsibility**. If Saturn plays a prominent role in your chart, the **south-west** direction can provide the stability and determination needed to reach the top in your career.

- **Jupiter's Influence**: Jupiter governs **growth** and **expansion**. If Jupiter is placed favorably in your birth chart, a workspace aligned with the **north-east** will promote growth and opportunities in your career or business ventures.

CASE STUDY: CAREER TRANSFORMATION THROUGH VASTU

Client: Mr. Suresh, a business owner, had been struggling with stagnation in his company's growth. Despite having a good product, his business was not expanding, and he faced challenges in attracting new clients and opportunities.

ANALYSIS:

Mr. Suresh's office had a **cluttered entrance** and his desk was placed in the **north-west** direction, which was leading to uncertainty and lack of focus.

The **south-east** area, which governs finance, was occupied with old furniture and unused items.

SOLUTION:

We moved his desk to the **north** to promote career advancement and prosperity.

The **south-east** was cleared and a **money plant** was placed in the area to attract financial success.

The **office entrance** was kept clear to ensure a smooth flow of energy.

OUTCOME:

Within a month, Mr. Suresh noticed an increase in business inquiries and a surge in client meetings. His company started to see new growth opportunities, and the overall energy in the office became more vibrant and focused.

CONCLUSION

Applying **Vastu Shastra** to your workspace can significantly impact your career and professional success. By understanding the power of directions, optimizing your workspace for positive energy flow, and incorporating **Astro Vedic** insights, you can create a productive, prosperous, and harmonious environment that supports your career growth. Whether you are an entrepreneur, a creative professional, or seeking advancement in your job, Vastu can be a powerful tool in your journey toward success.

CHAPTER 17: THE SCIENCE BEHIND VASTU SHASTRA AND ASTRO VEDIC PRINCIPLES

INTRODUCTION

While **Vastu Shastra** and **Astro Vedic** practices are deeply rooted in tradition, their underlying principles are based on natural laws, energy flows, and cosmic alignments. In this chapter, we delve into the scientific foundation of these practices, examining how the concepts of energy, space, and planetary influence work together to shape our environments and lives.

THE SCIENCE OF ENERGY AND VASTU SHASTRA

Vastu Shastra is not merely about architectural design or spatial arrangements; it is about the flow of energy and how different spaces interact with that energy. The core idea of Vastu lies in balancing the **five elements** (earth, water, fire, air, and space) within an environment to create a harmonious flow of energy that supports health, prosperity, and overall well-being.

1. THE FIVE ELEMENTS AND ENERGY FLOW

In **Vastu**, every space or structure is believed to be composed of the **five elements** (Panchabhutas). These elements have specific characteristics and play a crucial role in creating a harmonious environment. Each direction in Vastu corresponds to one of these elements, and the proper alignment of these elements in the home or office can lead to positive outcomes.

- **Earth (Prithvi)**: Governs stability, grounding, and nourishment. It is linked to the **south-west** and the foundation of any structure. Proper grounding of the building ensures that energy remains stable.

- **Water (Jal)**: Water represents flow, emotion, and wealth. It is associated with the **north-east** and brings fluidity and prosperity. Its placement in a structure influences health and abundance.

- **Fire (Agni)**: Fire represents energy, transformation, and passion. It is connected to the **south-east** and influences creativity, fame, and career growth.

- **Air (Vayu)**: Air governs communication, mobility, and change. It is associated with the **north-west** and ensures free movement of energy. Proper ventilation and air circulation improve the vitality of a space.

- **Space (Akasha)**: Space represents the soul of the structure and governs expansion and connectivity. It is linked to the **center of the building** and ensures the balance of all elements within the space.

The interaction of these elements in a building or environment determines the flow of energy. If the elements are in balance, they promote health, prosperity, and harmony. If they are imbalanced, they can cause obstacles, stress, and negative outcomes.

THE ROLE OF THE SUN AND MAGNETIC FIELD

One of the most scientifically significant aspects of Vastu is its consideration of natural forces such as the **sun** and the **Earth's magnetic field**.

1. THE SUN'S INFLUENCE

The **sun** is the most powerful source of energy for life on Earth. Vastu suggests that the placement of spaces and rooms according to the path of the sun can have profound effects on health, mood, and productivity. For instance:

- **South-facing windows** can bring in warmth and light, promoting activity and growth.

- **East-facing windows** are associated with morning sunlight, which is known to have a rejuvenating effect, helping with mental clarity and physical well-being.

These sun-based alignments also take into account the **time of day** and the **seasons**, which have different energies influencing various aspects of life.

2. EARTH'S MAGNETIC FIELD

The Earth's magnetic field influences the **north** and **south** directions. In **Vastu**, the **north** direction is associated with positive energy flow, as it aligns with the Earth's magnetic pole. This is why it is considered auspicious for key functions, such as sleeping, studying, or placing important documents.

The Earth's magnetic field also impacts our health. According to scientific studies, sleeping with your head to the **north** can disrupt the body's natural energy flow and interfere with restful sleep. This is why Vastu recommends placing the head to the **south** or **east** while sleeping.

ASTRO VEDIC SCIENCE AND PLANETARY INFLUENCE

Astrology, or **Astro Vedic**, takes into account the positions of the planets and their influence on human life. Just as Vastu Shastra governs the flow of energy in space, **Astro Vedic** governs the flow of energy through the individual, influenced by planetary placements in the birth chart.

1. THE IMPACT OF THE PLANETS

The nine planets in **Vedic astrology** influence our physical, mental, and spiritual well-being. Their positions at the time of our birth have lasting effects on various aspects of our lives, including health, career, relationships, and wealth.

- **Jupiter**: Associated with wisdom, prosperity, and expansion. Its influence is beneficial in the **north-east** of a home or office.

- **Saturn**: Known as the taskmaster, Saturn is linked to discipline, responsibility, and stability. The **south-west** direction is associated with Saturn, making it an ideal place for authority figures, leaders, and individuals seeking long-term growth.

- **Venus**: Venus governs beauty, creativity, and harmony. It is aligned with the **north-west** direction and enhances communication, socializing, and artistic expression.

- **Mars**: Mars represents strength, courage, and assertiveness. Its influence is linked to the **south-east**, which is ideal for activities related to ambition and success.

2. ASTROLOGICAL REMEDIES AND VASTU

Combining **Astro Vedic** insights with **Vastu** helps provide more personalized solutions. For example:

- If an individual's **Mercury** is weak in their astrological chart, placing items related to **Mercury** (like books, computers, or communication tools) in the **north** direction can help strengthen their abilities in communication and learning.

- Similarly, if **Saturn** is causing obstacles in one's career, adjusting the office space to align with **Saturn's** favorable zones (the **south-west**) can bring stability and positive energy.

THE SCIENTIFIC EXPLANATION OF VASTU FOR HEALTH AND WELL-BEING

The principles of **Vastu Shastra** are not just about spatial arrangement, but also about optimizing the flow of **life force energy**, also known as **Prana**. The layout of a building can impact the energy flow, affecting the health of the individuals living or working there.

1. ENERGY FLOW AND MENTAL HEALTH

A well-balanced environment leads to the proper flow of **Prana**, which positively affects mental clarity, emotional stability, and overall well-being. For example:

- **Cluttered spaces** hinder the flow of energy, leading to stress, anxiety, and poor mental health.

- **Open spaces** with natural light and good ventilation allow energy to circulate freely, improving mood and creativity.

2. THE ROLE OF WATER AND FIRE ELEMENTS IN HEALTH

Water, as an element, is strongly linked to the **north-east** in Vastu and represents healing and prosperity. A clean, well-maintained water feature in the **north-east** of a home or office can improve the energy flow, making the space more peaceful and conducive to well-being.

Similarly, **fire** in the **south-east** encourages vitality and enthusiasm. Ensuring that the fire element (such as a **stove**, **lamp**, or **candles**) is placed correctly can stimulate energy and drive.

CASE STUDY: THE SCIENTIFIC VALIDATION OF VASTU

Client: Mrs. Shalini, a wellness coach, was struggling with constant fatigue and a lack of motivation despite her passion for her career. Her office space was disorganized, with clutter in the **north-east** and no natural light coming in from the windows.

ANALYSIS:

Mrs. Shalini's office was a reflection of her internal state—disorganized and stagnant.

The **north-east** was blocked by a large bookshelf, which was restricting the flow of energy, and the windows faced the **west**, which meant they were receiving harsh afternoon sunlight.

SOLUTION:

We moved the bookshelf to a different location to open up the **north-east** corner, allowing energy to flow freely.

The desk was placed in the **north** direction to promote better clarity and energy flow.

We added plants near the **east-facing windows** to bring in natural light and fresh energy.

OUTCOME:

Within a few weeks, Mrs. Shalini reported an improvement in her energy levels, productivity, and overall mood. The changes in her workspace allowed her to connect with her clients better and run her wellness programs with renewed enthusiasm.

CONCLUSION

Both **Vastu Shastra** and **Astro Vedic** principles are based on the understanding of natural forces, energy flow, and cosmic alignments. These practices are deeply rooted in scientific principles, emphasizing the importance of balance, direction, and harmony in our lives. Whether applied to a building, workspace, or personal life, Vastu and Astro Vedic principles offer a comprehensive approach to enhancing health, prosperity, and success.

CHAPTER 18: INTEGRATING ASTRO VEDIC WITH MODERN LIVING

INTRODUCTION

In the modern world, where urbanization and fast-paced lifestyles dominate, many individuals seek ways to reconnect with the natural world and understand how the ancient sciences of Astro Vedic and Vastu Shastra can support their contemporary needs. This chapter explores how these age-old practices can be harmoniously integrated into modern living spaces and lifestyles for greater balance and prosperity.

THE NEED FOR BALANCE IN MODERN LIVING

Modern life often leads to an imbalance between the natural environment and human needs. Technology, work pressures, and urban living can disturb our natural rhythms, leading to stress, health issues, and a disconnect from our environment. The teachings of **Astro Vedic** and **Vastu Shastra** offer solutions by focusing on the **energies** in our surroundings and the **cosmic** influences on our lives.

1. TECHNOLOGY AND ENERGY FLOW

Technology has revolutionized our lives, but it has also introduced **electromagnetic fields (EMFs)**, radiation, and artificial lighting, which can disturb the natural flow of energy within our environments. In **Vastu Shastra**, the proper arrangement of a building can ensure that these modern elements don't block or disrupt the flow of energy.

SOLUTIONS:

- **Minimizing Electromagnetic Interference**: In a modern home, placing electronic devices such as computers, routers, and televisions in the right directions (preferably in the **south-west** or **south-east**) can help maintain energy balance.

- **Use of Natural Light**: **Natural sunlight** is a vital source of **Prana**. Incorporating **sunlight** through well-positioned windows in the **east** and **north** can counteract the artificial lighting that often dominates modern spaces.

2. BALANCING TECHNOLOGY WITH NATURE

Urban living spaces often lack elements that connect us to nature. Integrating nature into our spaces through **plants, natural materials**, and **water features** can bring the life-giving force of **Prana** into our environment.

SOLUTIONS:

- **Indoor Plants**: Plants are natural purifiers and bring life to spaces. Placing them in areas associated with the **north-east** or **east** can enhance energy flow and vitality.

- **Water Features**: Adding a **water fountain** or a **fish tank** in the **north-east** can promote calm and financial prosperity, as water is associated with wealth and vitality.

ALIGNING ASTRO VEDIC PRACTICES WITH CONTEMPORARY DESIGN

Designing a space that respects **Astro Vedic** and **Vastu** principles is achievable, even in modern structures that prioritize functionality and style. The key is to focus on balancing **cosmic energy** and aligning spaces to suit the individual's astrological needs.

1. PERSONALIZED DESIGN BASED ON ASTRO VEDIC CHART

Astrology plays a critical role in **Astro Vedic** practices, and understanding one's **birth chart** can influence design choices. Each person's chart dictates certain elements, colors, and placements that can harmonize with their **energetic** needs.

EXAMPLES:

- **East-facing Homes for Aries**: Those born under the **Aries** sign are ruled by **Mars**, and a **north-east** or **east-facing** entrance can enhance their fiery energy and leadership qualities.

- **North-west Locations for Libras**: Libras, ruled by **Venus**, benefit from a **north-west-facing** room where they can focus on relationships and harmony.

2. ARCHITECTURAL DESIGN WITH VASTU IN MIND

While modern architecture often leans toward open-plan concepts and minimalist design, incorporating **Vastu principles** does not require abandoning contemporary aesthetics. Simple adjustments like:

- **Room Placement**: Ensuring bedrooms are in the **south-west** for stability, or placing kitchens in the **south-east** for the fire element.

- **Directional Alignment**: Ensuring doors and windows open toward the **north** or **east** can allow natural energy to enter.

3. ASTROLOGICAL ADJUSTMENTS

If you know your client's astrological influences, designing their space around those principles can enhance the impact of your design. For instance, a **Leo** might benefit from a spacious, bold **south-facing** room to encourage confidence, while a **Taurus** might prefer a calm, grounded space in the **south-west** to support their need for stability.

OVERCOMING MODERN CHALLENGES WITH VASTU AND ASTRO VEDIC PRACTICES

Urban living often brings challenges such as **stress, pollution,** and a constant rush that can take a toll on physical and mental health. Both **Astro Vedic** and **Vastu Shastra** offer tools that can be used to overcome these modern challenges.

1. STRESS MANAGEMENT AND ENERGY FLOW

Stress is a prevalent issue in urban environments, and many people often feel overwhelmed due to clutter, poor energy flow, and environmental factors. **Vastu** provides solutions such as decluttering, proper lighting, and ensuring that key areas of the home are aligned with the correct **elemental energy**.

EXAMPLE:

- A cluttered **north-west** or **north-east** corner can cause tension and anxiety, while placing calming elements such as plants or water features can encourage relaxation and flow.

2. HEALTH AND WELL-BEING

Modern living often leads to **health problems** due to poor environmental conditions or lifestyle choices. By applying **Vastu principles**, we can create a healthier living space that nurtures the body and mind.

EXAMPLE:

- **Airflow**: Proper ventilation is key. Ensuring that the air can circulate freely through windows placed in the **east** and **north** will enhance health and energy levels.

CASE STUDY: CREATING A HARMONIOUS WORKSPACE

Client: Mr. Arvind, a businessman, was experiencing **declining productivity** and a **lack of motivation** in his office, despite having a modern and stylish workspace. He believed that his environment was contributing to his ongoing frustration.

ANALYSIS:

The office was located on the **top floor** of a modern building with **large windows** that faced the **west**, which allowed the harsh afternoon sun to flood the space. The **north-east** of the office was cluttered with filing cabinets and electrical equipment.

Mr. Arvind's birth chart revealed that he was an **Aquarius**, which benefits from a **south-east** facing desk and a **clear, open environment**.

SOLUTION:

We rearranged his desk to face the **south-east**, ensuring a better flow of energy. We cleared the clutter in the **north-east** and placed a **water fountain** in the corner to enhance prosperity and calmness.

Lighting: We added softer lighting and removed the bright, direct sunlight from the **west-facing** windows by using curtains that allowed diffused light to come through.

Plants: We placed indoor plants in the **east** and **north-east** corners to improve air quality and bring in positive energy.

OUTCOME:

After a week, Mr. Arvind reported increased focus and a sense of calm in the office. His team became more productive, and his overall motivation improved.

CONCLUSION

Integrating **Astro Vedic** principles and **Vastu Shastra** into modern living is not only feasible but also beneficial. By incorporating energy-balancing practices into our environments, we can counter the negative effects of modern life and create spaces that promote harmony, prosperity, and well-being. Whether it's by aligning rooms with **planetary influences**, improving **energy flow**, or simply **connecting with nature**, these ancient practices continue to offer relevant and practical solutions for contemporary challenges.

CHAPTER 19: VASTU SHASTRA AND ASTRO VEDIC: THEIR ROLE IN THE WORKPLACE

INTRODUCTION

In today's competitive and fast-paced world, the workplace has become more than just a space to perform tasks. It's a place that shapes our career, influences our productivity, and even impacts our overall well-being. By applying **Vastu Shastra** and **Astro Vedic** principles, business owners and employees can create a more balanced and prosperous work environment that enhances success and harmony.

The Impact of Space Design on Productivity

The design and layout of a workspace play a crucial role in the energy flow within the office. A well-designed workspace that adheres to **Vastu** principles promotes positive energy, creativity, and productivity, while an improperly designed space can cause stress, lethargy, and conflict.

1. VASTU AND THE OFFICE LAYOUT

In **Vastu Shastra**, different directions are associated with different elements and energies. For a workspace to be conducive to productivity and well-being, the office must be designed to promote a harmonious flow of these energies.

KEY ELEMENTS:

- **North-East**: The most auspicious direction in **Vastu**. It represents the **element of water**, bringing clarity, prosperity, and mental strength. This is the best location for **reception areas** or **important decision-making spaces**.

- **South-East**: This direction is associated with **fire** and represents the best place for your **office or work desk**. Fire stimulates energy, leadership, and determination.

- **South-West**: The **earth element** governs this direction, making it ideal for spaces requiring stability, such as **conference rooms** and **manager's offices**.

- **North-West**: Representing **air**, this is a dynamic space that supports **movement** and **communication**. Ideal for **sales teams** or **group workspaces**.

2. ENERGY FLOW AND MOVEMENT

Energy flow is crucial in ensuring that workspaces are aligned with **positive vibrations**. If the energy is stagnant or blocked, employees can experience fatigue, stress, and frustration.

SOLUTIONS:

- **Clutter-Free Zones**: Keeping the work environment **clutter-free** promotes **positive energy** and allows for better focus. The more organized the space, the smoother the energy flow.

- **Proper Furniture Placement**: The desk should be placed in a way that the employee can face the **north or east**, ensuring they are aligned with beneficial cosmic forces.

ASTRO VEDIC INSIGHTS FOR THE WORKPLACE

While **Vastu Shastra** deals with the physical layout and placement of objects within the office, **Astro Vedic** influences the alignment of these spaces according to an individual's **astrological birth chart**. This personalized approach can provide tailored recommendations for each individual to thrive in the workplace.

1. Astrological Alignments for Success

Each person's birth chart can influence their strengths, weaknesses, and best working conditions. By aligning a person's workspace with their **planetary influences**, it's possible to unlock their **full potential** and enhance productivity.

Example:

Capricorns (ruled by Saturn) benefit from a workspace that is **south-west** oriented, which enhances their natural **discipline** and focus.

Sagittarians (ruled by Jupiter) thrive in an **east-facing** workspace, promoting optimism and creativity.

2. PERSONALIZING THE WORKSPACE

Using an individual's **astrological profile**, the placement of their **work desk, furniture,** and even **decor** can be optimized to boost their success.

SOLUTIONS:

- **Gemstones**: Specific gemstones related to an individual's astrological sign can be placed on their desk to enhance focus and creativity.

- **Colors**: For instance, **blue** tones are excellent for **Pisces**, while **green** is best for **Tauruses** who need stability and grounding.

CASE STUDY: ENHANCING BUSINESS SUCCESS

Client: Mrs. Priya, a business owner in the **fashion retail industry**, was struggling with low employee morale and lack of productivity in her office. Despite having an aesthetically pleasing office, the energy in the space felt stagnant, and employees were constantly underperforming.

ANALYSIS:

- **Office Layout**: The office was located in the **north-west** section of the building, which is considered a good direction for communication, but the desks were placed in **poor positions**, facing away from the door.

- **Personalized Astro Vedic Assessment**: Mrs. Priya's birth chart revealed that she was a **Cancer** (ruled by the Moon), and she would benefit from a **north-facing desk** that nurtures creativity and intuition.

SOLUTION:

- We **re-arranged the desks** so that employees were facing **north** and **east**.

- The **conference room** was moved to the **south-west**, bringing stability to decision-making processes.

- **Astrological Adjustments**: We placed **white quartz** stones on the desks for calmness and balance, and adjusted the **color scheme** to reflect nurturing tones, like **light blue and green**.

OUTCOME:

Within weeks, employees reported feeling more motivated and connected to their work. Sales improved, and there was a noticeable boost in team collaboration and overall success.

BALANCING MODERNITY WITH TRADITION IN THE WORKPLACE

Modern office spaces often prioritize sleek, minimalistic designs, but this can sometimes come at the cost of energy balance. Applying **Vastu Shastra** and **Astro Vedic** principles doesn't mean compromising on modern aesthetics. In fact, the two can coexist beautifully, allowing for a workspace that is both stylish and energetically balanced.

1. Incorporating Natural Elements

Integrating **natural elements** such as plants, wood, and natural light can enhance the energy of the space. Plants are particularly beneficial when placed in the **north-east** corner to promote mental clarity and creativity.

2. SUSTAINABLE DESIGN CHOICES

Choosing sustainable materials that respect the environment also aligns with **Vastu** principles. For instance, using **wood** from renewable sources in furniture or **natural stones** can bring an added layer of harmony to the office space.

CONCLUSION

Creating a balanced and successful workplace requires more than just designing a space that looks good. By integrating the principles of **Vastu Shastra** and **Astro Vedic**, business owners can create an environment that promotes positive energy, productivity, and overall success. Understanding how to align spaces with the natural energies and planetary influences is essential for unlocking the true potential of any workplace.

CHAPTER 20: VASTU SHASTRA AND ASTRO VEDIC FOR HOMES: CREATING A HARMONIOUS LIVING SPACE

INTRODUCTION

Our home is not just a place where we live; it is a sanctuary that influences our physical, emotional, and spiritual well-being. In Vastu Shastra and Astro Vedic practices, the home is seen as a reflection of the balance between cosmic energies and personal forces. When the principles of these systems are applied correctly, they can transform a house into a space of peace, prosperity, and happiness.

THE ROLE OF VASTU IN CREATING A BALANCED HOME

Vastu Shastra focuses on the harmonious alignment of architectural elements with natural forces such as **earth**, **water**, **fire**, **air**, and **space**. Each of these elements plays a role in creating a balanced environment within a home.

1. VASTU AND THE HOME'S LAYOUT

The layout of your home has a direct impact on the flow of energy. When designed according to Vastu principles, your home can enhance health, wealth, and emotional well-being.

KEY VASTU CONSIDERATIONS FOR DIFFERENT AREAS OF THE HOME:

- **Entrance**: The main entrance of a house should ideally face the **north or east** to welcome positive energy. A door that faces the **south** or **south-west** may bring in negative energy.

- **Living Room**: The **north-east** corner of the house is ideal for the living room. This direction promotes clarity and harmony, setting a welcoming atmosphere for guests.

- **Bedroom**: The **south-west** corner is ideal for a master bedroom as it promotes stability and grounding, ensuring a restful night's sleep.

- **Kitchen**: The kitchen should be located in the **south-east** as it is governed by the **fire element**, which brings energy and vitality to meals and family gatherings.

2. HARMONIZING WITH THE FIVE ELEMENTS

Incorporating the five elements into your home design ensures a natural flow of positive energy. Using **natural materials** such as wood, stone, and clay can further enhance the balance within your living spaces.

EXAMPLE:

- **Water**: A **fountain** or **aquarium** in the **north-east** area of the house can promote calmness and prosperity.

- **Earth**: **Terracotta** or wooden flooring in the **south-west** corner brings grounding energy and stability to the bedroom.

- **Air**: Proper ventilation and an abundance of **natural light** in the home ensure the free movement of air, which is crucial for promoting a healthy environment.

ASTRO VEDIC: UNDERSTANDING THE ROLE OF ASTROLOGY IN HOME DESIGN

While Vastu Shastra focuses on the alignment of physical space, **Astro Vedic** brings in the influence of **astrology** to personalize the home environment for each individual. It considers the individual's **birth chart** to optimize their living space for better health, wealth, and harmony.

1. PERSONALIZED ASTROLOGY FOR HOME PLACEMENT

Each person's astrological birth chart plays a significant role in determining their best directions, energies, and even design elements. When creating a home, aligning the individual's birth chart with the **directional energies** can lead to an environment that supports their personal growth and success.

EXAMPLE:

Aries (Mars): Aries natives benefit from a **south-facing** room as Mars is associated with strength and assertiveness. Placing their **study desk** or **workstation** in the **south-west** can stimulate their drive for success.

Virgo (Mercury): Virgo natives are ruled by Mercury, the planet of communication and intellect. A **north-east** facing study or office space will help them thrive mentally and work effectively.

2. PLANETARY REMEDIES FOR THE HOME

Astro Vedic provides several remedies for balancing planetary influences within the home. These remedies may include the **placement of gemstones**, the use of specific **colors**, or the **installation of certain objects** in particular directions.

EXAMPLES:

- **Rahu and Ketu Remedies**: If **Rahu** or **Ketu** is poorly placed in a birth chart, placing a **tiger's eye gemstone** in the **south-west corner** can help reduce negative energy and promote balance.

- **Jupiter Remedies**: To enhance the positive influence of **Jupiter** (the planet of wisdom), placing **yellow flowers** or a **golden-colored object** in the **north-east corner** of the house will amplify intellectual growth and wealth.

CASE STUDY: THE TRANSFORMATION OF A HOME THROUGH VASTU AND ASTRO VEDIC

Client: Mr. Rajesh, a software engineer, was experiencing consistent struggles with his career and personal life. He was facing **low productivity**, a sense of **stagnancy**, and frequent disagreements with his family members.

ANALYSIS:

Mr. Rajesh's house was built without consideration of **Vastu** principles. The **kitchen** was located in the **north-west**, while his **work desk** was facing the **south-west**.

According to his **astrological birth chart**, Mr. Rajesh was born under the influence of **Saturn** and **Mercury**, and his **north-east direction** was his **lucky zone** for **personal growth** and **career**.

SOLUTION:

Vastu Adjustments: We moved the **kitchen** to the **south-east** corner and shifted the **work desk** to face **north**. This maximized the positive energy flow within the home.

Astrological Remedies: We introduced a **green jade gemstone** for **Mercury** to enhance communication and placed it in the **north-east corner** of the living room.

Personalization: We added a **yellow lamp** in the **north-east corner** of the living room to strengthen **Jupiter's** influence.

OUTCOME:

After the changes, Mr. Rajesh reported a significant improvement in his professional life. He received an unexpected promotion, and his productivity at work improved drastically. Family harmony was restored, and he felt more energized and positive about life.

THE IMPORTANCE OF CREATING BALANCE

Incorporating both **Vastu Shastra** and **Astro Vedic** principles into your home design helps create a **balanced** and **harmonious environment**. While **Vastu Shastra** addresses the broader physical space, **Astro Vedic** personalizes these designs to align with the unique energy of the individuals living within that space.

BALANCING TECHNOLOGY AND TRADITION

Today's modern homes are often filled with technological advancements, which can disrupt the natural energy flow of a house. However, balancing **technology** with **Vastu** and **Astro Vedic** principles can result in a space that embraces both modernity and tradition.

TIPS FOR MODERN HOMES:

- **Technology Placement**: Ensure that electronics such as **TVs**, **computers**, and **microwaves** are not placed in areas where they can disturb the **north-east** or **south-west** corners, as these are important for mental clarity and stability.

- **Use of Colors and Materials**: **Modern materials** such as **glass and metal** can be balanced with natural elements like **wood, stone**, and **fabric** to create harmony.

CONCLUSION

Designing a home that supports health, happiness, and prosperity requires a balance of both **Vastu Shastra** and **Astro Vedic** principles. By aligning your physical space with the cosmic energies and planetary influences, you can create a living environment that nurtures your well-being and enhances your future success.

CHAPTER 21: VASTU SHASTRA AND ASTRO VEDIC FOR WORKPLACES: CREATING PRODUCTIVE AND PROSPEROUS ENVIRONMENTS

INTRODUCTION

Just as the home is a reflection of the energies surrounding us, so too is the workplace. It's a space where our professional lives are nurtured and where success, growth, and innovation take shape. According to both **Vastu Shastra** and **Astro Vedic**, the design of a workplace can significantly impact productivity, relationships, and overall job satisfaction. By understanding how to align the physical environment with the flow of cosmic energy, businesses can create a space that promotes prosperity, creativity, and harmony among employees.

THE ROLE OF VASTU IN WORKPLACE DESIGN

Vastu Shastra offers a set of guiding principles that can be applied to any building, including workplaces. The right design and layout of a workspace can ensure a constant flow of positive energy, which will help employees to focus, collaborate, and excel in their work.

1. OFFICE LAYOUT AND DIRECTIONAL INFLUENCE

In Vastu Shastra, the layout of an office is crucial in determining how positive or negative energy will flow through the space. A well-designed office layout fosters collaboration, increases focus, and promotes productivity.

KEY VASTU CONSIDERATIONS FOR OFFICE SPACES:

- **Main Entrance**: Ideally, the entrance to an office should face the **north** or **east**. This direction is believed to bring prosperity and success, allowing positive energy to flow freely inside.

- **Manager's Office**: The **south-west** corner of the office is ideal for the manager's or owner's office. This position ensures stability, authority, and leadership energy.

- **Employee Desks**: Desks should ideally face **north** or **east** to enhance focus, efficiency, and mental clarity. The **south-west** direction is best for employees who handle financial matters or leadership roles.

- **Conference Room**: The conference room should be positioned in the **north-east** area, as this promotes clear thinking, creative discussions, and effective decision-making.

2. BALANCING THE FIVE ELEMENTS IN THE OFFICE

The five elements—**earth, water, fire, air,** and **space**—are fundamental in Vastu Shastra. When these elements are balanced correctly in the office space, they create an environment conducive to work and collaboration.

EXAMPLE:

- **Earth (Stability)**: In the **south-west** corner, using heavy furniture like solid wooden desks, bookshelves, or storage cabinets helps bring stability and grounding energy.

- **Water (Wealth)**: A **fountain** or **water body** in the **north** or **north-east** can enhance the flow of wealth and prosperity. It also helps reduce stress and brings calmness to employees.

- **Fire (Energy)**: The **south-east** direction is associated with the fire element. Introducing **bright lighting** or **natural sunlight** can stimulate creativity and energy in the workspace.

ASTRO VEDIC: USING ASTROLOGY TO ENHANCE THE WORKPLACE

Astro Vedic principles offer a personalized approach to workplace design by aligning the energies of the office space with the individual's astrological chart. By using astrology to determine the most favorable directions and elements for each individual, businesses can optimize employee performance and create a supportive work environment.

1. PERSONALIZED WORKPLACE DESIGN ACCORDING TO BIRTH CHARTS

Every employee's **birth chart** offers insights into their strengths, weaknesses, and ideal workspace environment. Aligning the workplace layout to the unique astrological needs of each individual can enhance their performance, motivation, and happiness.

EXAMPLE:

- **Taurus (Venus)**: Taurus employees, ruled by Venus, thrive in environments with luxury and comfort. The **south-east** corner, enriched with luxurious decor and natural elements, is ideal for them.

- **Capricorn (Saturn)**: Capricorn natives, governed by Saturn, excel in structured, disciplined environments. A **north-west-facing desk** will support their need for order and productivity.

2. ASTROLOGICAL REMEDIES FOR THE WORKPLACE

Astro Vedic also offers remedies for addressing the negative planetary influences within the office space. These remedies may include placing specific gemstones, using particular colors, or installing certain symbols or items that help counterbalance the effects of weak planetary influences.

EXAMPLES:

- **Mars Influence**: If Mars is negatively placed in the birth chart of an employee, placing a **red-colored object** in the **south-east** corner can calm down aggressive or impulsive tendencies.

- **Mercury Influence**: If Mercury is poorly placed in an employee's chart, using **green-colored decor** or a **jade gemstone** can enhance communication and mental clarity.

CASE STUDY: THE IMPACT OF VASTU AND ASTRO VEDIC ON A STARTUP'S SUCCESS

Client: A growing startup, **Tech Innovators**, was facing constant obstacles related to employee turnover, lack of productivity, and poor team dynamics. Despite having a creative and motivated workforce, the company was struggling to grow.

ANALYSIS:

The office layout was chaotic, with employee desks scattered without a clear organization, and the **conference room** was placed in a non-ideal location.

According to the birth charts of key team members, there was a significant influence of **Saturn** and **Rahu**, leading to delays, confusion, and lack of clarity.

SOLUTION:

Vastu Adjustments: The office layout was redesigned with **north-east** dedicated to the **conference room** for brainstorming and decision-making. Employees were moved to desks facing the **north** to enhance their focus and creativity.

Astro Vedic Remedies: **Mercury's** placement was problematic for the team leader, so a **green jade gemstone** was placed in their office to enhance communication. Additionally, **red-colored accents** were added to the **south-east corner** to help increase the team's energy.

OUTCOME:

After the adjustments, **Tech Innovators** saw an increase in **employee satisfaction**, with greater clarity in communication and collaboration. The company experienced a 25% growth in revenue within just a few months, and the team felt more motivated and aligned with their goals.

THE IMPORTANCE OF MAINTAINING THE RIGHT ENVIRONMENT IN THE WORKPLACE

The right workplace environment fosters the overall well-being of employees, leading to increased job satisfaction, greater productivity, and overall business success. By aligning the workplace design with **Vastu Shastra** and **Astro Vedic** principles, businesses can create a space that attracts positive energy, enhances relationships, and promotes success.

BALANCING MODERN WORKSPACES WITH TRADITIONAL WISDOM

In today's fast-paced work culture, it's easy to overlook the importance of a balanced workspace. However, by integrating traditional wisdom from **Vastu Shastra** and **Astro Vedic**, modern workspaces can be transformed into spaces of productivity, creativity, and prosperity.

TIPS FOR MODERN OFFICES:

Ergonomic Furniture: In addition to Vastu, ensuring **ergonomic furniture** can help employees maintain physical health, contributing to a more productive environment.

Technology Balance: While technology plays a significant role in the workplace, it's important to manage its influence on energy flow. Keep devices that generate electromagnetic fields, such as **computers** and **printers**, in areas where they don't disrupt the core **north-east** energy zone.

CONCLUSION

The office is an extension of an individual's energy, and just like a home, it can be influenced by both **Vastu Shastra** and **Astro Vedic** principles. By aligning the workspace with natural and astrological energies, businesses can create a productive, harmonious environment that encourages success and innovation. These adjustments, though subtle, have the power to improve employee morale, increase collaboration, and boost the business to new heights.

CHAPTER 22: USING ASTRO VEDIC AND VASTU SHASTRA FOR PERSONAL GROWTH AND SELF-IMPROVEMENT

INTRODUCTION

In the journey of life, personal growth and self-improvement are central to our well-being and success. While external circumstances can influence our path, there are tools and techniques that can help us harness our inner energy, improve our mental clarity, and guide us toward a fulfilling life. **Vastu Shastra** and **Astro Vedic** are ancient practices that can help individuals unlock their true potential by balancing their environment and aligning their energy with the cosmos. This chapter explores how these two powerful tools can be used for personal growth, focusing on the inner harmony and external support they offer.

ASTRO VEDIC FOR PERSONAL GROWTH

Astro Vedic is a branch of astrology that emphasizes the influence of celestial bodies on our lives, particularly how the positions of planets and stars can impact our personalities, behavior, and overall life trajectory. By understanding the astrological influences in our birth chart, individuals can gain insight into their strengths, weaknesses, and life's purpose.

1. UNDERSTANDING YOUR BIRTH CHART

Your **birth chart** is a snapshot of the sky at the time of your birth, showing the positions of the planets, sun, and moon. This chart acts as a map that reflects your inherent qualities, life path, and even the challenges you may face. Understanding your birth chart is one of the first steps in using **Astro Vedic** for self-improvement.

KEY ELEMENTS OF A BIRTH CHART:

- **Sun Sign**: Represents your core essence, ego, and identity. It reflects your fundamental nature and how you approach life.

- **Moon Sign**: Represents your emotions, mind, and inner self. It's crucial for understanding how you handle feelings and relationships.

- **Ascendant (Rising Sign)**: Represents your outward behavior and how others perceive you.

- **Planetary Positions**: The positions of planets in various houses reveal your strengths, challenges, and areas of potential growth.

By analyzing these elements, you can make informed decisions, avoid repeating past mistakes, and enhance your strengths.

VASTU SHASTRA FOR PERSONAL GROWTH

Vastu Shastra, as we've seen throughout the book, deals with the spatial arrangement and design of your living environment. The way your home is structured, the positioning of furniture, and even the colors you use can have a profound impact on your personal growth. By aligning your environment with the principles of **Vastu**, you can foster a sense of peace, stability, and positive energy that encourages self-improvement.

1. CREATING AN ENERGETICALLY BALANCED HOME

Your home is the foundation of your personal growth. It's where you retreat for rest, relaxation, and rejuvenation. The energy that circulates in your home can either help or hinder your progress. By adhering to **Vastu Shastra** principles, you can create an environment that supports growth and success.

KEY VASTU TIPS FOR PERSONAL GROWTH:

The Entrance: The main entrance to your home should face the **north** or **east**, bringing in fresh energy and setting a positive tone for your day.

The Bedroom: Your bedroom should ideally be in the **south-west** corner of the house, which promotes stability and deep rest. Sleep is essential for personal growth, as it rejuvenates both body and mind.

The Living Room: A well-lit, spacious living room encourages interaction and intellectual growth. The **north-east** corner is the most auspicious for this space, where natural light and air can circulate freely.

The Study Area: If you are working towards personal development or academic growth, the **north** or **east** direction is ideal for a study or work desk. This position enhances focus, learning, and clarity.

INTEGRATING ASTRO VEDIC AND VASTU FOR PERSONAL EMPOWERMENT

When used in tandem, **Astro Vedic** and **Vastu Shastra** create a holistic approach to personal growth, connecting your internal energies with the external environment. The combination of these two disciplines can accelerate your journey toward success, health, and happiness.

1. BALANCING PERSONAL AND EXTERNAL ENERGIES

While **Astro Vedic** focuses on understanding your internal energies (as defined by your birth chart), **Vastu Shastra** harmonizes the external energy of your environment. Aligning these energies leads to greater personal empowerment.

EXAMPLE:

If your **birth chart** shows that you are a strong communicator (possibly with a dominant **Mercury** influence), positioning your work or study space in the **north-east** corner will enhance your ability to articulate ideas and improve intellectual clarity.

Conversely, if your chart shows that **Saturn** (the planet of discipline) is weak, placing **metal objects** or playing with **Colours** in the **west** of your home can provide the stability and discipline needed for personal growth.

2. ASTROLOGICAL REMEDIES FOR PERSONAL GROWTH

Astrological remedies can help resolve obstacles in your personal life, whether they involve relationships, health, career, or finances. These remedies may include wearing specific gemstones, performing rituals, or meditating at particular times, all tailored to your unique astrological profile.

REMEDIES FOR PERSONAL GROWTH:

Gemstones: Wearing gemstones such as **Emerald** for Mercury (communication), **Ruby** for Sun (self-confidence), or **Blue Sapphire** for Saturn (discipline) can have a positive impact.

Mantras: Chanting specific mantras, such as the **Gayatri Mantra** or **Navagraha Mantras**, can help balance planetary influences and improve mental clarity and personal growth.

Yajnas (Fire Rituals): Certain fire rituals are believed to appease planets and cleanse negative energies, setting the stage for personal transformation.

CASE STUDY: TRANSFORMING PERSONAL LIFE WITH ASTRO VEDIC AND VASTU SHASTRA

Client: **Rajesh**, a 34-year-old businessman, was facing continuous obstacles in his personal and professional life. Despite his efforts, his business was not flourishing, and he felt stuck emotionally.

ANALYSIS:

Rajesh's **birth chart** showed an over-dominance of **Saturn**, which was leading to feelings of restriction and a lack of growth. Additionally, his home environment was chaotic, with clutter in the **north-east** corner and the bedroom positioned unfavorably in the **north-west**.

SOLUTION:

Astro Vedic Remedies: Rajesh was advised to wear an **emerald gemstone** to balance his Mercury, which governs communication and intellect. He was also encouraged to meditate in the **early morning hours** (the **Brahma Muhurta**) to harness positive energy.

Vastu Adjustments: The clutter in the **north-east** corner was cleared, and the bedroom was relocated to the **south-west**. The **north-east** was transformed into a study and meditation area to invite clarity and peace.

OUTCOME:

Within six months, Rajesh's business saw significant growth, and he reported feeling a sense of inner peace and motivation. His relationships improved, and he gained a clear direction in his personal and professional life.

CONCLUSION

The path to personal growth is a combination of inner awareness and external support. By integrating the principles of **Astro Vedic** and **Vastu Shastra**, individuals can align their inner energies with the cosmic forces and create an environment that fosters self-improvement and success. Whether it's improving relationships, boosting career growth, or enhancing mental clarity, these ancient sciences offer practical tools to help you achieve your full potential.

CHAPTER 23: THE ROLE OF VASTU SHASTRA AND ASTRO VEDIC IN BUSINESS AND CAREER SUCCESS

INTRODUCTION

Success in business and career doesn't come by chance; it is the result of a combination of factors, including strategic planning, hard work, and the alignment of energies. In many cultures, it is believed that the environment and cosmic influences play a significant role in determining the success or failure of ventures. **Vastu Shastra** and **Astro Vedic** are two ancient sciences that provide powerful insights into how external and internal energies can be harnessed for business and career success. This chapter explores how these two practices can influence and enhance one's professional life, promoting growth, prosperity, and stability.

ASTRO VEDIC FOR CAREER SUCCESS

Astro Vedic offers valuable insights into the optimal timing, direction, and strategies for career development. By understanding the positions of the planets at the time of one's birth, an individual can make informed career decisions and identify the best paths for growth and success.

1. ANALYZING YOUR BIRTH CHART FOR CAREER DIRECTIONS

Your **birth chart** can provide clear indications of which career paths are most aligned with your natural abilities. It reveals the strengths of different planetary positions, guiding you toward fields where you are likely to excel.

KEY PLANETS INFLUENCING CAREER:

- **Sun**: The Sun represents your self-confidence, leadership qualities, and professional identity. A strong Sun can indicate success in leadership roles, business ownership, and politics.

- **Mercury**: The planet of communication and intellect, **Mercury**, governs careers in writing, teaching, sales, and IT. A favorable Mercury indicates a sharp mind and the ability to influence others.

- **Venus**: Venus influences careers in the arts, beauty, fashion, and entertainment. A strong Venus suggests a talent for creative pursuits.

- **Saturn**: Saturn is the planet of discipline and hard work. A strong Saturn placement signifies success in careers requiring patience, perseverance, and organization, such as law, finance, or engineering.

- **Mars**: The planet of energy and ambition, **Mars**, governs careers in sports, military, entrepreneurship, and any field requiring physical energy or competitive spirit.

By analyzing your **birth chart**, an astrologer can help you identify the areas of strength and advise on which careers align best with your energies.

VASTU SHASTRA FOR BUSINESS SUCCESS

In addition to **Astro Vedic**, the practice of **Vastu Shastra** plays a significant role in ensuring that the physical environment supports growth, harmony, and prosperity. A business that is based in a space that follows the principles of **Vastu Shastra** is more likely to experience positive energy, increased productivity, and financial growth.

1. DESIGNING YOUR BUSINESS SPACE FOR SUCCESS

The layout, direction, and positioning of various elements within a business space are crucial in determining the flow of energy and the success of the business. Key elements of **Vastu Shastra** should be incorporated into your business premises to enhance prosperity.

VASTU TIPS FOR BUSINESS SUCCESS:

- **Main Entrance**: The **main entrance** to your business should face **north** or **east**. This allows positive energy to flow into the business, attracting success and prosperity. A clean, well-lit, and clutter-free entrance is essential to welcome good fortune.

- **Work Area**: The work area or office space should be positioned in the **north** or **east** of the building. These directions are associated with career growth, prosperity, and intellectual pursuits.

- **Cash Register or Financial Section**: The **cash register** should be placed in the **south-east** corner, as this is the direction associated with the element of **fire**, which represents wealth and abundance in **Vastu Shastra**.

- **Manager's Office**: The manager's or owner's office should ideally be located in the **south-west** corner of the building. This location enhances control, leadership, and stability, fostering a secure foundation for business growth.

- **Storage Area**: **Storage** and **inventory** areas should be placed in the **north-west** corner, as it ensures a smooth flow of stock and prevents any logistical or financial issues.

By ensuring that your business space is designed according to **Vastu** principles, you can create an environment that supports long-term success and stability.

CASE STUDY: BUSINESS GROWTH THROUGH ASTRO VEDIC AND VASTU SHASTRA

Client: **Anil**, a 42-year-old entrepreneur, faced stagnation in his business for several years. Despite his efforts, his sales were declining, and he felt disconnected from his work. His business premises did not seem to generate positive energy, and he frequently faced financial and logistical challenges.

ANALYSIS:

Astro Vedic Analysis: Anil's **birth chart** revealed a weak **Venus** placement, indicating challenges in the financial and creative aspects of his business. His **Mercury** was in a problematic position, hindering his ability to communicate effectively with clients and team members.

Vastu Analysis: Anil's business premises had several Vastu flaws: the main entrance faced the **south**, the manager's office was in the **north-east** corner, and the financial section was poorly placed in the **south-west**.

SOLUTION:

Astro Vedic Remedies: Anil was advised to wear a **diamond** (for Venus) and practice meditation to strengthen his **Mercury**. He was also encouraged to start networking with key influencers in his industry to attract more clients.

Vastu Remedies: The main entrance was repositioned to face **east**, and the manager's office was shifted to the **south-west**. The financial section was moved to the **south-east**, while the clutter in the business premises was cleared.

OUTCOME:

Within three months, Anil experienced a noticeable increase in sales, and his relationships with clients and employees improved. His business began to thrive, and he felt more connected to his work and motivated to pursue new opportunities.

INTEGRATING ASTRO VEDIC AND VASTU FOR HOLISTIC BUSINESS SUCCESS

By combining **Astro Vedic** and **Vastu Shastra**, entrepreneurs can create a business environment that is harmonious with both their internal energies and the external forces around them. This holistic approach leads to greater success, financial prosperity, and personal fulfillment in one's professional life.

1. TIMING IS EVERYTHING

Astro Vedic can also help determine the most auspicious times for business decisions. The placement of planets at specific times can influence everything from launching a new product to negotiating a deal. By consulting an astrologer for optimal timing, entrepreneurs can ensure that their efforts are aligned with cosmic support.

EXAMPLE:

If **Mars** is well-placed in your birth chart, it is a good time to launch a new product or start a marketing campaign. Similarly, if **Jupiter** is in a favorable position, it may be an ideal time to expand or invest in new ventures.

2. CREATING POSITIVE ENERGIES FOR BUSINESS GROWTH

By practicing both **Astro Vedic** and **Vastu Shastra**, business owners can ensure that their internal and external environments are aligned for success. This integrated approach offers a greater sense of stability, encourages financial growth, and attracts positive opportunities.

CONCLUSION

The success of a business is influenced by both internal and external factors. **Astro Vedic** provides valuable insights into an individual's strengths and challenges, while **Vastu Shastra** optimizes the environment to foster success and prosperity. By incorporating both practices into your business strategies, you can create a powerful combination that enhances productivity, financial growth, and overall well-being. This chapter has outlined how the alignment of energies, both personal and environmental, can contribute to business and career success. The next step is to integrate these principles into your own professional journey and watch as new opportunities unfold.

CHAPTER 24: THE IMPORTANCE OF VASTU SHASTRA AND ASTRO VEDIC IN HEALTH AND WELL-BEING

INTRODUCTION

Health and well-being are the foundation of a prosperous life. In our busy lives, we often overlook how our surroundings and the cosmic forces can affect our physical, mental, and emotional health. Both **Vastu Shastra** and **Astro Vedic** provide a holistic approach to health by balancing the energies within our bodies and the spaces we inhabit. This chapter delves into the role of these ancient practices in promoting good health, wellness, and harmony, ensuring that individuals lead balanced and fulfilling lives.

ASTRO VEDIC AND ITS IMPACT ON HEALTH

Astro Vedic offers valuable insights into how cosmic influences can impact one's physical and mental well-being. By understanding the alignment of planets and their effects on an individual's chart, Astro Vedic can provide recommendations to improve health and prevent diseases.

1. PLANETARY INFLUENCES ON HEALTH

Certain planets govern specific organs and parts of the body. By analyzing the position of these planets in a person's birth chart, astrologers can determine potential health issues and suggest remedies for maintaining wellness.

KEY PLANETS AND THEIR HEALTH IMPACTS:

- **Sun**: The Sun governs vitality, energy, and the heart. A weak Sun can lead to problems such as low energy, heart diseases, and fatigue. Strengthening the Sun through specific gemstones, colors, or mantras can improve overall health.

- **Moon**: The Moon influences the digestive system, mind, and emotions. An unfavorable Moon can cause digestive issues, mental instability, and emotional distress. Remedies for a weak Moon include meditation and using water-related healing methods.

- **Mars**: Mars governs the muscles, blood, and immune system. Imbalances in Mars can lead to issues with strength, accidents, or fevers. Wearing a red gemstone like coral and performing certain physical exercises can strengthen Mars.

- **Mercury**: Mercury is associated with the nervous system, lungs, and speech. A problematic Mercury can result in nervous disorders, respiratory issues, or speech-related problems. Strengthening Mercury can improve mental clarity and respiratory health.

- **Venus**: Venus governs the reproductive system, skin, and kidneys. Health problems related to Venus include skin disorders, infertility, and kidney-related issues. Wearing a diamond or engaging in creative activities can improve Venus-related health.

By analyzing the placement and aspects of these planets, Astro Vedic can offer preventive measures and lifestyle changes to avoid or mitigate health issues.

VASTU SHASTRA AND HEALTH

Vastu Shastra is not only about the design and layout of buildings, but it also emphasizes the balance of energies in the spaces we live and work in. A **Vastu-compliant** space can contribute significantly to physical, mental, and emotional health by ensuring that the flow of energies supports well-being.

1. VASTU AND ITS IMPACT ON HEALTH

The principles of **Vastu Shastra** dictate that the positioning of rooms, furniture, and elements such as water and light can influence the health of those living in the space. For example, poor placement of the bedroom, kitchen, or bathroom can lead to stress, poor sleep, digestive issues, and other health problems.

KEY VASTU TIPS FOR HEALTH AND WELL-BEING:

- **Bedroom Placement**: The **master bedroom** should be in the **south-west** direction. Sleeping with the head facing **south** is considered the best for a peaceful mind and good health. Avoid sleeping with the head facing **north**, as this can lead to health problems and disturbed sleep.

- **Kitchen Positioning**: The **kitchen** should ideally be in the **south-east** corner of the home, as this direction is associated with the element of **fire**, which governs digestion and metabolism. Placing the kitchen in the wrong direction can result in health problems, particularly related to the digestive system.

- **Bathroom and Toilet Placement**: Bathrooms and toilets should not be located in the **north-east** direction, as this can cause mental instability and digestive problems. They should be placed in the **west** or **north-west** directions to maintain a balance of energies.

- **Natural Light and Ventilation**: **Natural light** and **ventilation** play a crucial role in maintaining good health. The placement of windows and doors should allow sufficient sunlight to enter, especially in living rooms, bedrooms, and kitchens. Fresh air helps to reduce stress and improve mental clarity.

- **Indoor Plants**: The placement of **indoor plants** also plays a key role in health and well-being. Plants like **money plants, tulsi (holy basil), and aloe vera** have been known to purify the air, enhance oxygen levels, and reduce stress.

By following **Vastu** principles, individuals can create a home or office environment that is conducive to good health and well-being.

CASE STUDY: HEALTH TRANSFORMATION THROUGH VASTU AND ASTRO VEDIC

Client: **Reena**, a 35-year-old woman, was experiencing frequent headaches, anxiety, and digestive issues. Despite consulting several doctors, her condition didn't improve. She also felt emotionally drained and disconnected from her environment.

ANALYSIS:

- **Astro Vedic Analysis**: Reena's **Moon** and **Mercury** were found to be weak in her birth chart, contributing to her emotional instability, anxiety, and digestive issues. Her astrologer recommended wearing a **pearl** (for Moon) and engaging in regular **breathing exercises** to calm her nerves.

- **Vastu Analysis**: The analysis of Reena's home revealed several issues: her **bedroom** was facing **north**, and the **kitchen** was located in the **north-west**. These placements were disrupting her sleep cycle and digestion.

SOLUTION:

- **Astro Vedic Remedies**: Reena was advised to wear a **pearl** to strengthen the Moon and help her with emotional stability. She also began practicing **deep breathing** exercises and yoga to balance her mind and body.

- **Vastu Remedies**: Reena's bedroom was relocated to the **south-west** corner, and the bed was repositioned to face **south**. The kitchen was moved to the **south-east** corner, and the layout of her home was adjusted to improve energy flow.

OUTCOME:

Within two weeks, Reena experienced a significant improvement in her health. Her anxiety reduced, and she began sleeping better. Her digestive issues also subsided, and she felt more energetic and emotionally balanced.

INTEGRATING ASTRO VEDIC AND VASTU FOR HEALTH AND WELL-BEING

By integrating both **Astro Vedic** and **Vastu Shastra**, individuals can create a living environment that supports not just their physical health, but also their mental, emotional, and spiritual well-being. The key to a healthy life lies in the balance of internal energies (as indicated by **Astro Vedic**) and external energies (as governed by **Vastu Shastra**).

1. HOLISTIC HEALING

The combined influence of **Astro Vedic** and **Vastu Shastra** can help you achieve overall health and well-being by addressing both the internal (cosmic) and external (environmental) factors. This holistic approach to health can prevent illness, enhance vitality, and promote long-term wellness.

CONCLUSION

Your health is your most valuable asset, and taking proactive steps to ensure your physical, mental, and emotional well-being is essential for leading a fulfilling life. By utilizing **Astro Vedic** and **Vastu Shastra**, you can optimize your health by balancing the energies both within and around you. This chapter has outlined the importance of understanding the influence of the cosmos and the environment on your health. Through careful analysis and the application of remedies from both these sciences, you can improve your overall well-being and achieve a balanced, healthy life.

CHAPTER 25: HARMONIZING YOUR LIVING SPACE FOR PROSPERITY

INTRODUCTION

Prosperity is not just about wealth, but also about having a balanced and fulfilling life. A prosperous individual is someone who experiences success not just financially but also in their relationships, health, and overall life satisfaction. **Vastu Shastra** and **Astro Vedic** can both play a pivotal role in enhancing prosperity by creating a harmonious environment that fosters abundance and success. This chapter explores how aligning the energies of your home and personal space can significantly contribute to your prosperity.

THE ROLE OF VASTU IN PROSPERITY

Vastu Shastra helps in creating an environment that promotes prosperity by ensuring that energy flows harmoniously throughout your space. This is done by following certain principles related to space, direction, and the elements that can foster success, abundance, and positive energy.

1. VASTU AND PROSPERITY

Vastu dictates that the positioning of rooms and elements in your home or office plays a vital role in determining the prosperity you attract. Each direction governs a specific aspect of life, and by aligning your space with these natural forces, you can enhance your wealth and success.

KEY DIRECTIONS FOR PROSPERITY:

- **North**: The **north** is associated with **Kubera**, the lord of wealth in Hindu mythology. Placing important financial documents, a cash box, or wealth-related symbols in this direction can invite financial prosperity. It is also recommended to keep this area clutter-free and well-lit to encourage abundance.

- **South-East**: This direction is governed by the element of **fire** and is related to the **god of wealth**. The **south-east corner** of your home or office should ideally house the kitchen (as fire governs digestion) or a place of business. The element of fire also encourages the growth of personal wealth, so keeping this area vibrant and dynamic is key.

- **South-West**: The **south-west** governs stability and balance in life. A well-structured and calm space in this direction can help with long-term wealth accumulation and stability in personal and professional life. A **strong foundation** in this corner can be linked to long-term prosperity and success.

- **East**: The **east** is considered a direction of positive energy, connected to the sun. A well-lit, open area in the east ensures the inflow of creative energy and vitality, which can drive prosperity in all endeavors.

2. VASTU FOR FINANCIAL SUCCESS

Vastu suggests various practical steps that can be taken to improve your financial prospects. A few changes can make a world of difference in boosting prosperity.

- **Entrance Door**: The main entrance should be in the **north-east, north**, or **east** direction. This allows positive energy to enter the house and create a flow of prosperity. Ensure the entrance is clean, well-lit, and clutter-free.

- **Wealth Corner**: According to **Vastu**, the **south-east** or **north** corners of your home or office are excellent for placing wealth-related symbols such as coins, money plants, or crystals to enhance financial prosperity.

- **Avoid Clutter**: A cluttered or messy home can impede the flow of positive energy and hinder prosperity. Ensure that your home is neat and organized, with a special focus on the north-east area.

- **Mirror Placement**: A **mirror** placed in the **north** or **east** directions can enhance positive energy and help in attracting wealth. However, it should not reflect doors or windows as this may cause energy to escape.

ASTRO VEDIC INFLUENCE ON PROSPERITY

Astro Vedic influences the prosperity of an individual by understanding the planetary influences and aligning one's actions with the cosmic forces. The alignment of your birth chart with the right planetary transits and the right balance of **Karma** can have a profound effect on the prosperity you attract into your life.

1. PLANETARY ALIGNMENT FOR PROSPERITY

Certain planets are considered **benefic** for wealth and prosperity, while others might have a more challenging influence. The position of these planets at the time of birth, as well as during certain transits, can provide insights into financial success.

KEY PLANETS FOR PROSPERITY:

- **Jupiter (Guru)**: Known as the planet of wisdom and expansion, **Jupiter** is one of the most auspicious planets for wealth. Its favorable position in your birth chart indicates growth in all aspects of life, including prosperity.

Strengthening Jupiter through gemstones, mantras, or charitable activities can enhance your financial abundance.

- **Venus (Shukra)**: Venus governs material comforts, wealth, and prosperity. A well-placed Venus ensures good fortune in business, finances, and relationships. Remedies for an afflicted Venus include wearing a **diamond** or performing rituals on Fridays.

- **Saturn (Shani)**: While **Saturn** is often associated with challenges, its position can also guide you toward long-term, sustainable prosperity. Understanding how Saturn influences your chart can help you align your work efforts with time-tested success.

- **Mars (Mangala)**: Mars represents energy, motivation, and courage. A strong Mars can help you take bold actions in your career and finances, leading to prosperity. Conversely, a weak Mars may cause delays and obstacles. Regular **exercise** and **assertiveness** can help strengthen Mars.

- **Rahu and Ketu**: These shadow planets govern **uncertainty**, **changes**, and **unseen influences**. Their placement can indicate periods of financial instability or change. However, when aligned with the right energies, they can also bring sudden wealth.

2. ASTRO REMEDIES FOR PROSPERITY

- **Mantras and Gemstones**: Specific **mantras** can help strengthen planets that govern prosperity, such as the **Jupiter Mantra** or **Venus Mantra**. Wearing gemstones like **yellow sapphire** for Jupiter or **diamond** for Venus can attract financial success.

- **Yagyas and Rituals**: Performing certain **Vedic rituals**, such as **Lakshmi Pujas, Satyanarayan Katha,** or offering prayers on auspicious days, can help bring prosperity into your life.

- **Charity and Giving**: One of the most powerful Astro Vedic remedies for prosperity is **giving**. Donating to the less fortunate, especially on specific days related to your birth chart, can enhance the flow of positive energy into your life.

CASE STUDY: PROSPERITY TRANSFORMATION THROUGH VASTU AND ASTRO VEDIC

Client: **Rajesh**, a 45-year-old businessman, was struggling to attract financial success despite putting in long hours of work. He felt stagnant in his business and was unable to find new opportunities. His home and office felt heavy, and his financial situation was getting worse over time.

ANALYSIS:

- **Astro Vedic Analysis**: Rajesh's **Jupiter** was weak in his birth chart, indicating a lack of growth in his career and financial life. His **Venus** was also poorly placed, contributing to the lack of material success. He was advised to wear a **yellow sapphire** to strengthen Jupiter and to perform regular **Venus-related rituals**.

- **Vastu Analysis**: Rajesh's office was located in the **north-west** direction, which is not ideal for a business environment. The main entrance of his home was in the **south-west** direction, blocking the inflow of positive energy.

SOLUTION:

- **Astro Vedic Remedies**: Rajesh wore a **yellow sapphire** to strengthen Jupiter and performed **Lakshmi Pujas** to enhance his financial situation. He was also advised to increase his **charitable activities**, especially on Thursdays, to increase the flow of wealth.

- **Vastu Remedies**: Rajesh's office was relocated to the **north** direction, and the entrance to his home was shifted to the **north-east** corner. He also added **money plants** and **crystals** to the north-east area of his home.

OUTCOME:

Within three months, Rajesh experienced a noticeable improvement in his financial situation. New business opportunities started coming in, and his profits grew. His home and office felt lighter, and he was more positive and motivated.

CONCLUSION

Creating an environment that promotes prosperity is not just about financial wealth; it is about attracting abundance in all areas of life. By aligning your space with **Vastu Shastra** and ensuring that your personal energies are in harmony with the **cosmic forces** through **Astro Vedic** remedies, you can cultivate a life of wealth, success, and fulfillment. The practices outlined in this chapter are not only about improving financial circumstances but also about creating a harmonious, balanced, and prosperous life.

CHAPTER 26: AN CASE STUDY OF VASTU COMPLIANT OFFICE

CASE STUDY: M/S. D.M. & ASSOCIATES, ITANAGAR, ARUNACHAL PRADESH

When M/s. D.M. & Associates approached us in Itanagar, Arunachal Pradesh, we were presented with a rare and exciting opportunity—an entirely blank canvas. The site was undeveloped and devoid of structural limitations, offering us the freedom to plan from the ground up. Our mission: to design a workspace that was not only functional and efficient but also aligned with Astro Vedic and Vastu principles to ensure harmony, prosperity, and productivity.

INITIAL SITE ANALYSIS

Our first step was a detailed site analysis using the 16-direction method. We studied the topography, soil quality, natural slopes, and orientation of the land. Based on the magnetic north and the client's business nature, we identified ideal directional alignments for each functional area.

PLANNING FROM SCRATCH – A VASTU-CENTRIC APPROACH

With complete architectural freedom, we incorporated the following Astro Vedic Vastu elements:

- **Main Entrance**: Positioned in the East as well as East-NorthEast (Eshanya) zone to attract positive cosmic energy and facilitate growth in professional endeavors.

- **Reception & Waiting Area**: Located in the NorthEast to benefit from the morning sunlight, promoting warmth and welcoming vibes.

- **Managing Partner's Cabin**: Designed in the South-West (Nairutya), symbolizing strength, control, and stability in decision-making.

- **Staff Workstations**: Oriented in the North-NorthWest (Vayavya), allowing flexibility and movement, ideal for departments requiring dynamism.

- **Toilets**: Carefully restricted to the West-NorthWest to maintain energetic balance.

- **Pantry & Refreshment Area**: Situated in the Soth of South-west, the zone of fire, ideal for kitchen and heating elements.

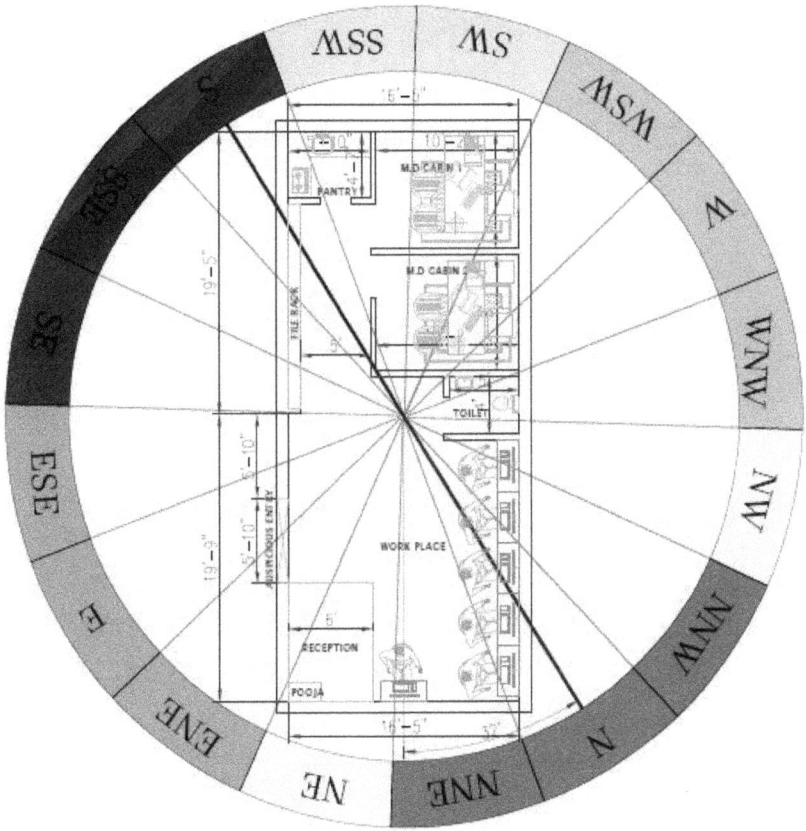

DISTRIBUTION OF 16 ZONES AND FIVE ELEMENTS

ENTRANCE FALL ON JAYANT & INDRA PADA, THIS PADAS ARE AUSPICIOUS FOR MAIN ENTRY.

32 ENTRANCE DISTRIBUTION

ASTROLOGICAL SYNCHRONIZATION

We also consulted the birth charts of the managing partners to fine-tune directional recommendations. Special attention was given to the planetary influences on professional success and team harmony. Specific materials, colors, and interior elements were selected based on favorable planetary alignments.

OUTCOME

The project now stands as a benchmark of Astro Vedic-Vastu integration. Since its completion, M/s. D.M. & Associates has reported:

- Improved team cohesion and workplace satisfaction

- Enhanced client inflow and timely project completions

- Fewer internal conflicts and a generally calm, focused work atmosphere

This project demonstrates how blending ancient wisdom with modern design practices can result in an environment that supports both tangible business success and intangible wellbeing.

CHAPTER 27: CONCLUSION: THE PATH TO PROSPERITY

INTRODUCTION

As we conclude this book on **Astro Vedic in Vastu Shastra**, we have explored the vast realms of ancient wisdom that combine the energies of the universe with the science of space to create a balanced, harmonious life. Both **Vastu Shastra** and **Astro Vedic** offer valuable insights into how the energies around us shape our fate, influence our prosperity, and impact our overall well-being.

In this concluding chapter, we reflect on the key concepts we've covered, summarize the practical steps that can be taken, and remind ourselves of the powerful transformation that can occur when we align our lives with these ancient sciences.

THE ROLE OF ASTRO VEDIC AND VASTU SHASTRA IN OUR LIVES

1. A SYNERGY OF TWO ANCIENT SCIENCES

Vastu Shastra and **Astro Vedic** are not standalone practices but are deeply interconnected. While **Vastu** focuses on creating a physical environment that supports prosperity and well-being by aligning spaces with natural forces, **Astro Vedic** helps us understand how the cosmic forces, particularly the positions of planets and stars, influence our personal and professional lives. Together, these two sciences provide a comprehensive framework to bring harmony, wealth, health, and success into every aspect of life.

2. PRACTICAL APPLICATION

It's one thing to know the principles of these sciences, but it is quite another to apply them in our everyday lives. The key to success is consistency and conscious effort. Implementing **Vastu principles** in your home or workspace, such as organizing your space according to the cardinal directions, keeping clutter at bay, and ensuring proper placement of essential elements, can lead to a significant positive shift in your surroundings. Likewise, understanding and harnessing the **Astro Vedic** influence of planets can help you make informed decisions, from selecting auspicious times for important events to remedies that empower you to unlock new levels of success.

3. TRANSFORMING YOUR FUTURE

The integration of **Astro Vedic** and **Vastu** provides an opportunity to shape a future that is abundant in wealth, good health, and spiritual well-being. Every individual has the power to influence their destiny by aligning their physical space and astrological influences with the principles shared in this book. Whether you are looking to build a prosperous business, improve your health, or strengthen relationships, the combined energies of Vastu Shastra and Astro Vedic can help guide your path.

THE KEY TAKEAWAYS

Vastu Shastra is the science of architecture and design that helps align your physical environment with the forces of nature. It governs the positioning of rooms, furniture, and the flow of energy in a way that supports your well-being and prosperity.

Astro Vedic looks at the cosmic influences, the positioning of planets, and their impact on your personal life. By understanding the energy of the stars and planets, you can take actions that align with their beneficial influences.

Prosperity is not just about financial wealth, but about creating a harmonious balance in all areas of life—health, relationships, career, and spirituality. Both **Vastu** and **Astro Vedic** work together to help you achieve this balance.

Practical Remedies include using the correct placement of rooms and elements, aligning your personal actions with the right astrological timings, and making use of gemstones, mantras, and rituals to enhance your personal growth.

Consistency is key. Prosperity and peace are not achieved overnight. With continued effort and dedication to living in harmony with the natural forces around you, you can ensure a prosperous future.

FINAL THOUGHTS

The journey towards prosperity is deeply personal and unique to each individual. However, the principles of **Astro Vedic** and **Vastu Shastra** offer universal guidance to align yourself with the energies that govern success. By applying the insights you have gained from this book, you are not only transforming your surroundings but also harnessing the cosmic forces that shape your destiny.

Whether you're redesigning your home or seeking clarity on your astrological chart, remember that prosperity is the result of balanced actions and environments. By taking the time to nurture your space and understanding the planets' influence, you are setting the stage for a prosperous future.

As we wrap up this exploration, know that both **Vastu Shastra** and **Astro Vedic** are lifelong studies. Continue to delve into these sciences, seek further wisdom, and apply them in your daily life to continue your journey toward health, wealth, and happiness.

A NOTE OF GRATITUDE

We express our heartfelt gratitude to **Vishal Agarwal**, whose dedication to the study of **Astro Vedic** and **Vastu Shastra** has paved the way for the creation of this book. His contributions, knowledge, and commitment to sharing these insights with the world are truly invaluable.

We hope this book has illuminated your path and provided the tools to bring prosperity and harmony into your life.

CONCLUSION: MOVING FORWARD

We leave you with the timeless wisdom of **Vastu Shastra** and **Astro Vedic**, encouraging you to apply these teachings with dedication. By doing so, you will find that prosperity is not just a dream but a reality waiting to unfold.

This concludes the book on **Astro Vedic in Vastu Shastra**. Thank you for joining us on this transformative journey. May your life be filled with peace, prosperity, and endless possibilities.

www.ingramcontent.com/pod-product-compliance
Lightning Source LLC
Chambersburg PA
CBHW022130080426
42734CB00006B/303